INTERNAL AUDIT
CAPABILITY MODEL (IA-CM)
FOR THE PUBLIC SECTOR

Overview and Application Guide

INTERNAL AUDIT
FOUNDATION™

The IIA's International Professional Practices Framework (IPPF) comprises the full range of existing and developing practice guidance for the profession. The IPPF provides guidance to internal auditors globally and paves the way to world-class internal auditing.

The IIA and the Foundation work in partnership with researchers from around the globe who conduct valuable studies on critical issues affecting today's business world. Much of the content presented in their final reports is a result of Foundation-funded research and prepared as a service to the Foundation and the internal audit profession. Expressed opinions, interpretations, or points of view represent a consensus of the researchers and do not necessarily reflect or represent the official position or policies of The IIA or the Foundation.

The Internal Audit Foundation based the structure of this model, in part, on "CMMI® for Development, Version 1.2," CMU/SEI-2006-TR-008, copyright 2006 Carnegie Mellon University, with special permission from the Software Engineering Institute.

ANY MATERIAL OF CARNEGIE MELLON UNIVERSITY AND/OR ITS SOFTWARE ENGINEERING INSTITUTE CONTAINED HEREIN IS FURNISHED ON AN "AS-IS" BASIS. CARNEGIE MELLON UNIVERSITY MAKES NO WARRANTIES OF ANY KIND, EITHER EXPRESSED OR IMPLIED, AS TO ANY MATTER INCLUDING, BUT NOT LIMITED TO, WARRANTY OF FITNESS FOR PURPOSE OR MERCHANTABILITY, EXCLUSIVITY, OR RESULTS OBTAINED FROM USE OF THE MATERIAL. CARNEGIE MELLON UNIVERSITY DOES NOT MAKE ANY WARRANTY OF ANY KIND WITH RESPECT TO FREEDOM FROM PATENT, TRADEMARK, OR COPYRIGHT INFRINGEMENT.

This model has not been reviewed nor is it endorsed by Carnegie Mellon University or its Software Engineering Institute.

CMMI is a registered trademark of Carnegie Mellon University.

ISBN-13: 978-1-63454-009-4
21 20 19 18 17   1 2 3 4 5 6

Printed in Canada

CONTENTS

Executive Summary vii

Preface xi

Acknowledgments xiii

About the Authors xv

I.   Overview 1

    1.   Introduction 1

        1.1   Background 1

    2.   Internal Auditing and the Environment 2

        2.1   Internal Audit Guidance 3

        2.2   Environment 4

    3.   The IA-CM in Summary 5

        3.1   What is the Public Sector IA-CM? 5

        3.2   The Structure of the IA-CM 7

        3.3   KPAs by Internal Audit Element 19

    4.   Selected Bibliography 27

    Annex A: Original Research Purpose, Methodology, and Onsite Validations 31

        A.1 Research Purpose and Methodology 31

        A.2 Onsite Validations 32

II. Application Guide—The IA-CM in Detail 37

    1.   Introduction 37

    2.   The IA-CM in Detail 37

        2.1   The IA-CM One-Page Matrix 37

        2.2   The Elements of Internal Auditing 40

        2.3   The Capability Levels—Descriptions and Relationships among KPAs 43

3.   **Applying and Interpreting the IA-CM** 60

    3.1   Principles in Applying the IA-CM 60

    3.2   Environmental and Organizational Factors 60

    3.3   Capability Level Issues. 60

    3.4   The IA-CM and a Quality Assurance and Improvement Program 61

4.   **Detailed Key Process Areas** 64

    Services and Role of Internal Auditing. 65

    People Management 71

    Professional Practices. 82

    Performance Management and Accountability 90

    Organizational Relationships and Culture 99

    Governance Structures 104

Annex B: Examples Using the IA-CM. 112

    B.1   Self-Assessment, Continuous Improvement, and Capacity Development 112

    B.2   Internal Assessment (Standard 1311) 118

    B.3   Visioning and Communication Tool. 120

    B.4   Strategic Planning. 123

    B.5   Benchmarking. 126

Internal Audit Foundation Sponsor Recognition 129

Internal Audit Foundation Board of Trustees 131

Internal Audit Foundation Committee of Research and Education Advisors. 132

LIST OF EXHIBITS

Exhibit I.1: IA-CM Levels 7

Exhibit I.2: Descriptions of the Capability Levels 8

Exhibit I.3: Elements of Internal Auditing 11

Exhibit I.4: Descriptions of the Elements of Internal Auditing 11

Exhibit I.5: Internal Audit Capability Model Matrix 15

Exhibit I.6: Mastering a KPA 17

Exhibit I.7: Institutionalizing a KPA 18

Exhibit I.8: Purposes of KPAs by Internal Audit Element 19

Exhibit A.1: IA-CM Validation Sessions with IA Activities 32

Exhibit A.2: Other IA-CM Validation Input 35

Exhibit II.1: Internal Audit Capability Model Matrix 39

Exhibit II.2: Elements of Internal Auditing 40

Exhibit II.3: IA-CM Levels 43

Exhibit II.4: Assessment of Government Environment 45

Exhibit II.5: Purposes of the KPAs at Level 2—Infrastructure 48

Exhibit II.6: Purposes of the KPAs at Level 3—Integrated 52

Exhibit II.7: Purposes of the KPAs at Level 4—Managed 56

Exhibit II.8: Purposes of the KPAs at Level 5—Optimizing 58

Exhibit II.9: Excerpts from Standards 1300 – 1312 62

Exhibit II.10: Key Process Area 64

EXECUTIVE SUMMARY

The Internal Audit Capability Model (IA-CM) was published in September 2009 by the Internal Audit Foundation (formerly The Institute of Internal Auditors Research Foundation). It is a framework that identifies the fundamentals needed for effective internal auditing in the public sector and consists of five progressive capability levels tied to practices demonstrated at each level. In line with the principle-based nature of internal auditing, the IA-CM is not intended to be prescriptive in terms of how a process should be carried out. More important is its use in assessing whether the internal audit (IA) activity is appropriately established to realize its desired capability level.

In 2009, governments were acknowledging the critical importance of internal auditing in enhancing the economy, efficiency, and effectiveness of all levels of public sector administration. Now internal auditing is seen as an integral part of good governance. Internal audit stakeholders, in mature organizations, understand the benefits of internal audit as an independent assurer of effective organizational governance, risk management, and control processes; a trusted advisor dynamically responding to emerging risks and management concerns; and a leader encouraging the importance of risk and control considerations in the first and second lines of defense.

> Today internal auditors are seen as an integral part of good governance, independent assurers, trusted advisors, and leaders who encourage the importance of risk and control considerations.

In 2016, the Foundation agreed that internal audit professionals and their stakeholders would benefit from aligning the IA-CM with current and evolving practices, and highlighting real-life experiences where the IA-CM is currently used to strengthen the maturity and improve the effectiveness of internal auditing. It was also agreed that a common assessment tool for applying the IA-CM would be useful.

Since its original publication, external environmental issues, internal audit professional practices, and business and risk management have evolved. The conceptual base of the IA-CM remains sound and internal audit practitioners around the world are still effectively using the model.

Annex B in this publication includes detailed examples from internal audit professionals where the IA-CM is currently being used for self-assessment and continuous improvement, capacity development, strategic planning, visioning and communication, and benchmarking. Examples highlighted include IA activities from Asia, Africa, North America, South America, and Europe and range from mature to less mature functions and from governments using the model to a one-person shop in the United States.

For example, the Republic of Indonesia's central Government Internal Auditor has used the IA-CM since 2010 to improve government-wide capabilities of internal auditing. In 2016, The IIA–Netherlands adapted the IA-CM to its environment and published an Internal Audit Ambition Model (IA-AM). A Fortune 500 Retailer in the United States began using the model in 2010 and continues to use the IA-CM as a tool for developing its overall internal audit strategy and conveying its vision to senior management and the audit committee. Several IA activities in Canada have applied the IA-CM to facilitate the performance of their Quality Assurance and Improvement Programs through a periodic Quality Assurance Review, further to Standard 1311 – Internal Assessments. In this way, the IA-CM adds value as a communication tool, self-assessment tool, and performance improvement tool and has been invaluable in ensuring that internal audit capabilities are aligned with the organization's expectations.

Furthermore, the 2016 United Nations Joint Inspection Unit's report, *State of the Internal Audit Function in the United Nations System*, states that "A good practice observed in a few organizations in the United Nations system, including UNRWA and WFP, and also in the Organisation for Economic Co-operation and Development (OECD), was the use of the IIA Internal Audit Capability Model as a means of gauging the desired level of maturity of the internal audit function. Determining the desired maturity level can guide the development of the internal audit strategy." (Paragraph 84, page 20)

It was through consultation with such past and present users of the IA-CM, global internal audit thought leaders, and extensive literature review of current and evolving environmental influences and professional practice guidance that the IA-CM has been updated. It now reflects leading developments in governance, business and risk management, and the internal audit profession to ensure that it is relevant, useful, practical, and forward-thinking.

To refresh the IA-CM, the context was reviewed in detail and revisions were made throughout the entire publication, including the detailed key process areas (KPAs), to reflect current and evolving professional developments, practices, and innovative concepts, such as:

- The IIA's International Professional Practices Framework (IPPF)
  - o Mission of Internal Audit (2015)
  - o Core Principles for the Professional Practice of Internal Auditing (2015)
  - o Revisions to the *International Standards for the Professional Practice of Internal Auditing* (up to and including January 2017)
  - o Recommended Guidance, comprised of Implementation Guidance and Supplemental Guidance (including applicable Practice Guides issued since 2009)
  - o Results of the 2010 and 2015 CBOK Studies

- Committee of Sponsoring Organizations of the Treadway Commission's (COSO's) 2013 *Internal Control - Integrated Framework*, updated in response to increased expectations from stakeholders regarding governance, risk management, and fraud prevention.

- Internal audit's increased alignment with the organization's business and risk management practices, including internal audit's role and relationship with control and risk functions in an organization's three lines of defense.

- Internal audit's enhanced leveraging of knowledge management systems and information technology to improve implementation of internal audit professional practices and increase effectiveness and efficiency.

- The importance of fostering and strengthening internal audit stakeholder relationships to help build confidence in the work of internal audit and demonstrate its responsiveness to the needs of the organization.

With respect to the IA-CM itself, the framework remains the same in terms of the five progressive capability levels, the six elements of internal auditing, and its 41 KPAs. The IA-CM continues to be seen as a universal framework that identifies the fundamentals needed for effective internal auditing in the public sector. It illustrates the levels and stages through which an IA activity can evolve as it defines, implements, measures, controls, and improves its processes and practices. It describes an evolutionary path for public sector organizations to follow in developing effective internal auditing to meet the organization's needs and professional expectations.

However, the rapid pace of change in business and operating environments has necessitated changes in the practice of internal auditing, as has been the increased expectations with respect to the value that internal auditors should deliver to their organizations.

To reflect those changes, contextual revisions have been made throughout the publication and the descriptions of the capability levels, and the definitions of the six elements have been augmented to incorporate current practices. Further, during the review of the detailed KPAs, revisions were made to the essential activities, outputs, outcomes, and institutionalizing practice examples, as necessary, to reflect evolving expectations and practices. References to The IIA's mandatory and recommended guidance are also included, as relevant.

Three KPAs, in particular, have been changed to better reflect the current environment.

In Level 5 – Optimizing, within the Performance Management and Accountability element, the title of the KPA has changed from "Public Reporting of IA Effectiveness" to "Outcome Performance and Value to Organization Achieved" to emphasize the importance of a world-class IA activity at Level 5 meeting all stakeholders' expectations of value to the organization. The corresponding purpose, essential activities, outputs, and institutionalizing practice examples have changed accordingly.

> Three KPAs in particular have been changed to better reflect the current environment.

In Level 3 – Integrated, within the Governance Structures element, the title of the KPA has changed from "Management Oversight of the IA activity" to "Management Oversight and Support of the IA Activity" to emphasize management's role in supporting and facilitating the work of the IA activity without compromising the independence of the function. The purpose of this KPA has also been revised slightly to better reflect this concept.

One KPA in Governance Structures has been moved from Level 4 – Managed to Level 3 – Integrated: "IA Activity Reports to Top-level Authority" to reflect the current practice where more public sector IA activities are in fact reporting to the board, as defined by The IIA.

Further, to assist in understanding the viability of establishing an IA activity, that is to say, assessing the likelihood that internal audit can move from Level 1 to Level 2 – Infrastructure, an exhibit has been added that identifies seven attributes/key features in a government environment that may impact on the capacity to implement internal auditing in a lasting and effective way.

This publication is now augmented by a comprehensive assessment tool available electronically, to assist IA activities and their stakeholders effectively apply the IA-CM. As such, in addition to its use as a self-assessment and continuous improvement model for IA activities, the IA-CM can be used by senior management, stakeholders, and legislators to evaluate the need for and the type of IA activity appropriate for their organizations or jurisdictions and develop a strategy for achieving the desired capability for the IA activity. Further, it can be used as a tool to advocate the importance of internal auditing to stakeholders and decision makers.

PREFACE

The IA-CM is a framework that identifies the fundamentals needed for effective internal auditing in the public sector. It describes an evolutionary path for a public sector organization to follow in developing effective internal auditing to meet the organization's governance needs and professional expectations. The IA-CM shows the steps in progressing from a level of internal auditing typical of a less established organization to the strong, effective, internal audit capabilities generally associated with a more mature and complex organization. The IA-CM also provides guidelines/strategies to assist the IA activity develop attributes and achieve objectives beyond simply meeting professional standards.

The IA-CM is:

- **A communication vehicle**—a basis for communicating what is meant by effective internal auditing and how it serves an organization and its stakeholders, and for advocating the importance of internal auditing to decision makers.

- **A framework for assessment**—a framework for assessing the capabilities of an IA activity against professional internal audit standards and practices, either as a self-assessment or an external assessment.

- **A road map for orderly improvement**—a road map for building capability that sets out the steps an organization can follow to establish and strengthen its IA activity.

The IA-CM provides a **tool** that a public sector organization can use to:

- Determine its internal audit requirements according to the nature, complexity, and associated risks of its operations.

- Assess its existing internal audit capabilities against the requirements it has determined.

- Identify any significant gaps between those requirements and its existing internal audit capabilities and work toward developing the appropriate level of internal audit capability.

A number of **principles** underlie the IA-CM:

- Internal auditing is an integral component of effective governance in the public sector and helps organizations achieve their objectives and account for their results.

- Three variables must be considered when assessing the level of capability of an IA activity—the activity itself, the organization, and the overall environment in which the organization operates.

- An organization has an obligation to determine the optimum level of internal audit capability to support its governance needs and to achieve and maintain the desired capability.

- Not every organization requires the same internal audit capability or sophistication. The appropriate level will be commensurate with the nature and complexity of the organization and the risks to which the organization may be exposed. "No one size fits all."

- The capability of the IA activity is directly related to the actions taken by the chief audit executive (CAE) to establish the processes and practices needed to achieve and maintain the internal audit capabilities and the measures taken by the organization's management to establish a supportive environment for internal auditing.

- Internal auditing must be delivered in a cost-effective manner.

The IA-CM is intended as a universal model with comparability around principles, practices, and processes that can be applied globally to improve the effectiveness of internal auditing. In line with the principle-based nature of internal auditing, this model is not intended to be prescriptive in terms of how a process should be carried out.

The IA-CM publication comprises three sections—an Overview of the IA-CM, an Application Guide, and an Online Assessment Tool.

The Overview provides background on the research project itself, some environmental and contextual information about internal auditing, and a description of the model, including its underlying principles and structure. A selected bibliography is provided. Also included, as an Annex in the Overview, is the original research purpose, methodology, and onsite validations.

The Application Guide describes the IA-CM in detail—its elements, capability levels, KPAs, and how to use and interpret the model. It describes the capability levels in detail and identifies the relationships among KPAs found in the elements at the progressive capability levels. For each of the 41 KPAs, the purpose, essential activities, outputs, and outcomes are identified along with examples of institutionalizing practices that support mastering and institutionalizing the KPA. Some examples of current uses of the IA-CM are also included as an Annex.

The IA-CM Online Assessment Tool provides guidance in applying the IA-CM as an assessment instrument. The Assessment Tool includes a structured methodology for assessing the capabilities of an IA activity against the expectations set out in the IA-CM. The Assessment Tool can be used in a couple of ways:

- As a tool for the IA activity to develop strategies for strengthening its capability and improving its effectiveness.

- As an external assessment vehicle that results in the provision of an opinion to senior management or the board on the capabilities of the IA activity.

The Online Assessment Tool can be accessed using the following link: **www.theiia.org/IA-CM**

ACKNOWLEDGMENTS

The Internal Audit Foundation wishes to express its appreciation to the review team from the Committee of Research and Education Advisors (CREA) who supported the current revision of the IA-CM. It would like to thank the current IA-CM users who contributed to the revision and those that agreed to share their experiences using the model in Annex B of this current publication. The Foundation also wishes to express its appreciation to all those who participated in the original development and validation of the IA-CM for the Public Sector, including:

- The Internal Auditing Department of the World Bank for its financial support and technical expertise working with the research team to validate the IA-CM globally.

- The IA activities and others, identified in Exhibits A.2.2.1 and A.2.2.2, that participated during the global validations of the IA-CM.

- The volunteer internal audit professionals on the IA-CM review team:

  o Brian Aiken, CIA, CFE, Assistant Comptroller General, Treasury Board Secretariat, Canada
  o Jacques Lapointe, CA, CIA, CGAP, Auditor General of Nova Scotia, Canada
  o Bruce Sloan, CA, Senior Principal, Office of the Auditor General of Canada
  o Colleen Waring, CIA, CGAP, former Deputy City Auditor, City of Austin, Texas, USA

- The following institutes and committees for helping coordinate the IA-CM validations during 2008: IIA–Argentina, IIA–Australia, IIA–Croatia, IIA–Egypt, IIA–France, IIA–Kenya, IIA–Malaysia, IIA–Tanzania, IIA–United Kingdom, IIA–Uganda, the Foundation's Committee of Research and Education Advisors (CREA), and The Institute of Internal Auditors' (IIA's) Public Sector Committee (PSC).

- Carnegie Mellon University and its Software Engineering Institute for providing permission to use its CMMI® for Development, Version 1.2 as the basis, in part, for the structure of this model.

ABOUT THE AUTHORS

Elizabeth (Libby) MacRae, CGAP, was the lead researcher and principal author of the Internal Audit Foundation's publication *Internal Audit Capability Model (IA-CM) for the Public Sector*. She has also co-authored with Diane van Gils, PhD, two additional Foundation reports: *Internal Audit Capabilities and Performance Levels in the Public Sector* and *Nine Elements Required for Internal Audit Effectiveness in the Public Sector*. She has extensive internal audit practitioner experience developed through her more than 30 years in the Government of Canada where she held three chief audit executive (CAE) positions. She was also a senior research associate with the Canadian Comprehensive Audit Foundation (CCAF), a Canadian research and education foundation. She has been a member of The IIA for more than 25 years, during which time she was president of the Ottawa Chapter, a member of the Vision for the Future Task Force, the Professional Issues Committee, the Internal Audit Standards Board, the Public Sector Committee, and Common Body of Knowledge (CBOK) 2015 Practitioner Subcommittee. She is also the chairperson of a United Nations Audit Committee, which provides her with experience in international and public sector governance, risk management, and accountability.

Bruce C. Sloan, CPA, CA, CRMA, has extensive public sector experience developed through more than 30 years in the Government of Canada, where he served with the Office of the Auditor General leading a broad range of performance audits, including many government-wide assessments of internal audit within the Canadian federal government. He has been a member of The IIA for more than 25 years, during which time he was president of the Ottawa Chapter, a member of the Committee on Quality, the Professional Issues Committee, and the Public Sector Committee. He currently serves as a member of the Guidance Development Committee. He was a member of the review team for the Internal Audit Foundation's publication *Internal Audit Capability Model (IA-CM) for the Public Sector*.

I. OVERVIEW

1. Introduction

The Overview provides a high-level summary of the Public Sector Internal Audit Capability Model (IA-CM). It includes background on the original research project itself, some current environmental and contextual information about internal auditing, and a description of the model, including its underlying principles and structure. An updated selected bibliography is also provided.

1.1 Background

The IA-CM was published in September 2009. It is a framework that identifies the fundamentals needed for effective internal auditing in the public sector and consists of five levels, tied to practices demonstrated at each level.

Since its original publication, external environmental issues, internal audit professional practices, governance, and business and risk management practices have evolved. The conceptual base of the IA-CM remains sound and practitioners around the world are still effectively using the model. However, leading developments in governance, business and risk management, and the profession need to be reflected in the IA-CM to ensure that it is current and relevant.

In 2016, the Foundation agreed that internal audit professionals and their stakeholders would benefit from aligning the IA-CM with current practices; highlighting examples of real-life experiences where the IA-CM has been used to strengthen the maturity and improve the effectiveness of internal auditing; and developing a common assessment tool for applying the IA-CM.

By way of background, The IIA's Public Sector Committee (PSC) recommended in 2004 that an IA-CM be developed to reinforce the importance of internal auditing in public sector governance and accountability. It recognized that internal auditing could vary significantly from country to country because of differences in management practices, processes, and culture of a particular government. The PSC identified the need for a universal model that public sector IA activities could use as a self-assessment and development tool to assess their progress and determine training and capacity-building needs.

At that same time, governments at all levels—national, regional (provincial or state), and local (county or city)—were acknowledging the critical importance of internal auditing in enhancing the economy, efficiency, and effectiveness of all levels of public sector administration. There was clearly a need for a universal public sector governance model that included internal auditing.

In September 2006, the Foundation approved the project to develop an IA-CM to be used globally to help evolve public sector internal auditing by strengthening its capability and improving its effectiveness. The model is based on an adaptation of the Software Engineering Institute's Software Capability Maturity Model® that was developed as a tool for assessing an organization's ability to build software applications and the more recent Technical Report, "CMMI® for Development, Version 1.2."[1]

Today, the IA-CM continues to be seen as a universal framework that identifies the fundamentals needed for effective internal auditing in the public sector. It illustrates the levels and stages through which an IA activity can evolve as it defines, implements, measures, controls, and improves its processes and practices. It describes an evolutionary path for public sector organizations to follow in developing effective internal auditing to meet the organization's needs and professional expectations.

> Today, the IA-CM continues to be seen as a universal framework that identifies the fundamentals needed for effective internal auditing.

In addition to its use as a self-assessment and continuous improvement model for IA activities, the IA-CM has been used by senior management, internal audit stakeholders, and legislators to evaluate the need for and the type of IA activity appropriate to their organizations or jurisdictions, taking into consideration the roles and responsibilities within the different lines of defense.[2]

This model can also be used by national, regional, and local legislative auditors as a source of benchmarks. They could report to legislators on the extent to which any given public sector IA activity has reached maturity in terms of governance, policy and practices framework, organization and structure, resources, and services.

Details of the original IA-CM research purpose, methodology, and global validations performed are found in Annex A of the Overview.

2. Internal Auditing and the Environment

This section sets the context for the IA-CM by providing some commonly accepted definitional and contextual information relating to internal auditing. It also introduces some current environmental and organizational factors that may impact on the capability and evolution of an IA activity. These are expanded on in the Application Guide.

---

[1] CMMI®, CMM®, and Capability Maturity Model® are registered in the U.S. Patent and Trademark Office.

[2] The Three Lines of Defense model describes responsibilities for effective risk management and control as follows: management is primarily responsible for monitoring and controlling processes, and is the first line of defense in risk management; the second line of defense consists of separately established risk, control, and compliance oversight functions that ensure properly designed processes and controls are in place within the first line of defense and are operating effectively; the nature and types of these functions are dependent on many factors, including industry and organizational maturity; functions, such as internal audit, that provide independent assurance over processes and controls are considered the third line of defense. The IIA Position Paper "The Three Lines of Defense in Effective Risk Management and Control" (Lake Mary, The Institute of Internal Auditors, 2013.)

2.1 Internal Audit Guidance

Effective in 2015, The IIA promulgated the Mission of Internal Audit, which describes what internal audit seeks to achieve: "To enhance and protect organizational value by providing risk-based and objective assurance, advice, and insight."

To achieve that mission, "Internal auditing is an independent, objective assurance and consulting activity designed to add value and improve an organization's operations. It helps an organization accomplish its objectives by bringing a systematic, disciplined approach to evaluate and improve the effectiveness of risk management, control, and governance processes." (The IIA's globally accepted definition of internal auditing)

Also, in 2015, The IIA articulated the Core Principles for the Professional Practice of Internal Auditing (Core Principles), which are the key elements that describe internal audit effectiveness.

Internal auditing is performed by professionals with an in-depth understanding of the organization's business culture, systems, and processes. Internal auditors are expected to adhere to The IIA's mandatory guidance, which includes the Definition of Internal Auditing, the *International Standards for the Professional Practice of Internal Auditing (Standards)*, the 10 Core Principles, and the Code of Ethics.

In addition to the mandatory guidance identified in The IIA's International Professional Practice Framework (IPPF),[3] Recommended Guidance is included, which comprises Implementation Guidance and Supplemental Guidance. It is through such guidance that the professionalism of internal auditing can be demonstrated along with its value to the organization.

"The operation of the IAA [IA activity] is complex and demanding. The CAE [chief audit executive] must manage both internal and external relationships, the administration and organization of the activity, the plan and functioning of the audits performed, and resolve any issues that may arise."[4]

The foregoing statement was made in the *Global Summary of the Common Body of Knowledge 2006* (CBOK). While it is still applicable, external environmental issues, internal audit professional practices, and business and risk management have evolved since that time.

A publication from the 2015 CBOK now emphasizes increased complexity in the business environment and internal audit's potential contribution. "The ever-increasing complexity of business in an always-on, globally connected world means that there is a growing list of ways that internal auditors can deliver value to their organizations. They can provide assurance over specific aspects of the business, offer insights and recommendations to maximize return on organizational activities, and present objectivity to decision makers—all of which deliver on internal audit's value proposition ...of assurance, insight, and objectivity."[5]

---

[3] The IPPF is the conceptual framework that organizes authoritative guidance published by The IIA.

[4] *A Global Summary of the Common Body of Knowledge 2006* (Lake Mary, FL: The Institute of Internal Auditors Research Foundation, 2007), 239.

[5] Jane Seago, *Delivering on the Promise: Measuring Internal Audit Value and Performance* (Lake Mary, FL: The Institute of Internal Auditors Research Foundation, 2016), 4.

Specifically with respect to the public sector, the "three value propositions [protector, educator, advisor] are not mutually exclusive and they are anchored in the unique attributes and assets that the audit profession brings to the public sector table. These include professionalism, trustworthiness, independence, objectivity and robust methodologies."[6]

The needs and expectations of stakeholders cannot be overemphasized. "To be perceived to add value, the IAA [IA activity] must strategically align the needs and priorities of all its key stakeholders, including the AC [audit committee], executive management, and external auditors."[7]

The IA activity works collaboratively with management and the oversight body to provide assurance that governance processes are effective and efficient, internal controls are adequate to mitigate the organization's risks, and organizational goals and objectives are met.

2.2 Environment

Internal auditing is a global profession and is practiced in both the public and private sector. As such, it is conducted in diverse legal and cultural environments; within organizations that vary in purpose, size, complexity, and structure; and by persons within or outside the organization. Such differences impact on the practice of internal auditing.

In determining the most appropriate IA activity for an organization in the public sector, it is important to consider the influence that corporate governance structures, risk management, and control frameworks have on the ability to implement internal auditing and develop the necessary internal audit capabilities.

"Government is becoming more challenging and unpredictable: interdependencies are numerous and relationships with stakeholders are increasing in number, diversity, and complexity… Expectations for accountability and stewardship are on the rise."…[8]

Organizations are increasingly referring to the Three Lines of Defense model to address such interdependencies and higher expectations for accountability and stewardship.

As such, "…Driven by oversight requirements and eroding public trust, there are ever more players in the public sector mandated to assess, review, examine, and opine on government operations and performance. They include a range of management and management advisory functions such as program evaluation and risk management which are mandated to measure government results and risks respectively. As well, individual departments and ministries have various internal compliance functions in place, tasked to assess and attest to the department's conformity to internal policies, controls, or quality expectations. Examples here include compliance and quality functions related to regulatory oversight activity, transfer payment management, or administrative activities such as staffing and procurement. In many jurisdictions, the monitoring and oversight role of the chief

---

[6] Carmen Abela and James R. Mitchell, *Unlocking the Power of Internal Audit in the Public Sector*, The Institute of Internal Auditors Canada, 2014, vii.

[7] *A Global Summary of the Common Body of Knowledge 2006* (Lake Mary, FL: The Institute of Internal Auditors Research Foundation, 2007), 376.

[8] Carmen Abela and James R. Mitchell, *Unlocking the Power of Internal Audit in the Public Sector* (The Institute of Internal Auditors Canada, 2014), 2.

financial officer is increasing in scope and authority. Added to this are the myriad external functions that play an increasingly active role in assessing and overseeing government operations. Among the most notable of these are the legislative auditors, mandated to audit financial statements and to audit the effectiveness, efficiency, and economy of departments…"[9]

The Three Lines of Defense model is also often used to organize and align the players in this public sector regime.

In addition, the reality that management capacity, infrastructure, and governance arrangements are different in developed and developing countries must also be considered. Furthermore, when introducing measures to strengthen internal auditing in developing and transitional countries, it is necessary to understand different audit traditions and institutional capacities.

It is important to look at the receptiveness of a particular country to financial management reforms. Factors to be considered include government stability and culture, appetite for reform, the legislative system, the maturity of corporate governance, the tradition and practices of external audit, and whether there are central drivers for internal auditing.

In this respect, it is important to note the established authority and role of the Supreme Audit Institution in a particular country, its professional practices, and its relationship with internal auditing—whether it is seen as complementary to internal auditing or has assumed internal audit's role.

There may be real capacity constraints that impact on implementing internal auditing in a particular environment or restrict the IA activity to a less evolved capability level. In some developing and transitional countries, it may not be possible to generally conform with the *Standards* in view of environmental and political factors. For example, if the environment has not fully embraced organizational and individual accountability for results, it may be difficult for internal auditing to progress to a mature and effective IA activity.

3. The IA-CM in Summary

3.1 What is the Public Sector IA-CM?

The IA-CM is a framework that identifies the fundamentals needed for effective internal auditing in the public sector. It describes an evolutionary path for a public sector organization to follow in developing effective internal auditing to meet the organization's governance needs and professional expectations. The IA-CM shows the steps in progressing from a level of internal auditing typical of a less established organization to the strong, effective, internal audit capabilities generally associated with a more mature and complex organization. The IA-CM also provides guidelines/strategies to assist the IA activity develop attributes and achieve objectives beyond simply meeting professional standards.

The IA-CM is:

- **A communication vehicle**—a basis for communicating what is meant by effective internal auditing and how it serves an organization and its stakeholders, and for advocating the importance of internal auditing to decision makers.

---

[9] Ibid, 3.

- **A framework for assessment**—a framework for assessing the capabilities of an IA activity against professional internal audit standards and practices, either as a self-assessment or an external assessment.

- **A road map for orderly improvement**—a road map for building capability that sets out the steps an organization can follow to establish and strengthen its IA activity.

The IA-CM provides a **tool** that a public sector organization can use to:

- Determine its internal audit requirements according to the nature, complexity, and associated risks of its operations.

- Assess its existing internal audit capabilities against the requirements it has determined.

- Identify any significant gaps between those requirements and its existing internal audit capabilities and work toward developing the appropriate level of internal audit capability.

A number of **principles** underlie the IA-CM:

- Internal auditing is an integral component of effective governance in the public sector and helps organizations achieve their objectives and account for their results.

- Three variables must be considered when assessing the level of capability of an IA activity—the activity itself, the organization, and the overall environment in which the organization operates.

- An organization has an obligation to determine the optimum level of internal audit capability to support its governance needs and to achieve and maintain the desired capability.

> The IA-CM is a framework for strengthening or enhancing internal auditing through many small evolutionary steps.

- Not every organization requires the same internal audit capability or sophistication. The appropriate level will be commensurate with the nature and complexity of the organization and the risks to which the organization may be exposed. "No one size fits all."

- The capability of the IA activity is directly related to the actions taken by the chief audit executive (CAE) to establish the processes and practices needed to achieve and maintain the internal audit capabilities and the measures taken by the organization's management to establish a supportive environment for internal auditing.

- Internal auditing must be delivered in a cost-effective manner.

The IA-CM is intended as a **universal model** with comparability around principles, practices, and processes that can be applied globally to improve the effectiveness of internal auditing. In line with the principle-based nature of internal auditing, this model is not intended to be prescriptive in terms of how a process should be carried out. More important is its use in assessing whether the IA activity is established to realize its desired capability level.

3.2 The Structure of the IA-CM

The IA-CM is a framework for strengthening or enhancing internal auditing through many small evolutionary steps. These steps have been organized into five progressive capability levels. The model illustrates the stages through which an IA activity can evolve as it defines, implements, measures, controls, and improves its processes and practices.

Improvements in processes and practices at each stage provide the foundation on which to progress to the next capability level. Hence, it is a "building block" approach to establishing effective internal auditing in an organization. A fundamental premise underlying the IA-CM is that a process or practice cannot be improved if it cannot be repeated. It is therefore not sustainable.

3.2.1 Capability Levels

The five levels of the IA-CM are:

1. Initial
2. Infrastructure
3. Integrated
4. Managed
5. Optimizing

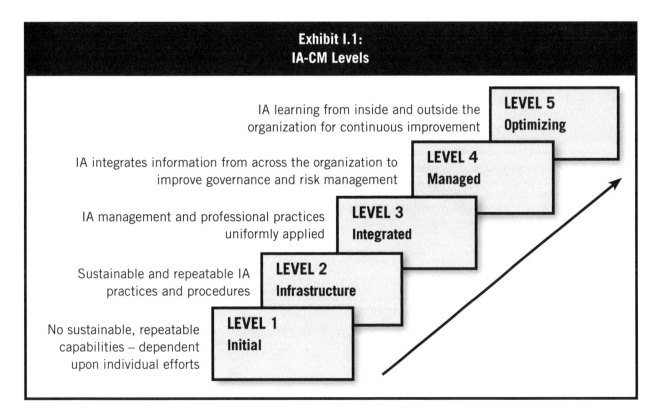

Exhibit I.1:
IA-CM Levels

LEVEL 5 Optimizing — IA learning from inside and outside the organization for continuous improvement

LEVEL 4 Managed — IA integrates information from across the organization to improve governance and risk management

LEVEL 3 Integrated — IA management and professional practices uniformly applied

LEVEL 2 Infrastructure — Sustainable and repeatable IA practices and procedures

LEVEL 1 Initial — No sustainable, repeatable capabilities – dependent upon individual efforts

Each capability level describes the characteristics and capabilities of an IA activity at that level (see **exhibit I.1**). As either the size or complexity of an organization or the risks associated with its operations increases, so does the need for more sophisticated internal audit capabilities. The model attempts to match the nature and complexity of an organization with the internal audit capabilities needed to support it. In other words, if the organization requires a greater degree of sophistication in internal audit practices, the IA activity will typically be at a higher capability level. The internal audit capability level is often tied to the governance structure of the organization within which it is situated.

> The IA-CM attempts to match the nature and complexity of an organization with the IA capabilities needed to support it.

The capability levels in the model provide a road map for continuous improvement within the IA activity. However, an IA activity may choose to remain at any level and that level may be the most appropriate for that IA activity in that particular organization and environment.

For example, an IA activity may wish to remain at a particular level and improve the efficiency and quality of implementation of the processes at that level by establishing "better practices," rather than necessarily striving for and evolving to a higher capability level. Another factor to consider in this respect is the "cost to improve"—to move from Level 2 to Level 3 or from Level 3 to Level 4. In other words, an IA activity may choose to remain at Level 2 or Level 3, and not aspire to a higher capability level because the current level is the most cost effective at that particular point in time. In addition, other uncontrollable factors, such as local regulations, may preclude a particular IA activity from fully embracing a higher level.

Furthermore, IA activities need to regularly monitor their capability level and review the essential activities and processes established to sustain that level. The IA activity needs to ensure that it continues to address environmental, organizational, and stakeholders' needs such that internal audit continues to provide continuous insight, assurance, and advice.

Summary descriptions of the levels are found in **exhibit I.2**.

Exhibit I.2: Descriptions of the Capability Levels	
5 – Optimizing	– IA is a trusted advisor.
	– IA is a learning organization with continuous process improvements and innovation.
	– IA uses information from inside and outside the organization to contribute to achieving strategic objectives.
	– World-class/recommended/best practice performance.
	– IA is a critical part of the organization's governance structure.
	– Top-level professional and specialized skills.
	– Individual, unit, and organizational performance measures are fully integrated to drive performance improvements.

Exhibit I.2: (continued) **Descriptions of the Capability Levels**	
4 – Managed	– IA and key stakeholders' expectations are in alignment. – Performance metrics are in place to measure and monitor IA processes and results. – IA is recognized as delivering significant contributions through value-added services to the organization. – IA has developed a framework broad enough to encompass risk and control considerations at all levels of the organization's governance, risk management, and control processes. – IA functions as an integral part of the organization's governance and risk management. – IA is a well-managed business unit. – Risks are measured and managed quantitatively. – Requisite skills and competencies are in place with a capacity for renewal and knowledge sharing (within IA and across the organization).
3 – Integrated	– IA policies, processes, and procedures are defined, documented, and integrated into each other and the organization's infrastructure. – IA management and professional practices are well established and uniformly applied across the IA activity. – IA is starting to align with the organization's business and the risks it faces. – IA evolves from conducting only traditional IA to integrating as a team player, conducting performance or process-based auditing, and providing advice on performance and management of risks. – Focus is on team building and capacity of the IA activity and its independence and objectivity. – IA supports the implementation and coordination of an effective Three Lines of Defense model. – Generally conforms with the *Standards*.
2 – Infrastructure	– Key question or challenge for Level 2 is how to establish and maintain repeatability of processes and thus a repeatable capability. – IA reporting relationships, management and administrative infrastructures, and professional practices and processes are being established (IA guidance, processes, and procedures). – Audit planning is based principally on management priorities. – Continued reliance essentially on the skills and competencies of specific persons. – Conducts principally compliance or controls-based auditing. – Partial conformance with the *Standards*.

Exhibit I.2: (continued) **Descriptions of the Capability Levels**	
1 – Initial	– Ad hoc or unstructured.
	– Isolated single audits or reviews of documents and transactions for accuracy and compliance.
	– Outputs dependent upon the skills of the specific person holding the position.
	– No professional practices established other than those provided by professional associations.
	– Funding approval by management, as needed.
	– Absence of infrastructure.
	– Auditors likely part of a larger organizational unit.
	– Institutional capability is not developed.

3.2.2 Elements of Internal Auditing

The following six essential elements were identified for an IA activity:

1. Services and Role of Internal Auditing
2. People Management
3. Professional Practices
4. Performance Management and Accountability
5. Organizational Relationships and Culture
6. Governance Structures

The first four elements—Services and Role of Internal Auditing, People Management, Professional Practices, and Performance Management and Accountability—relate primarily to the management and practices of the IA activity itself. The last two elements—Organizational Relationships and Culture and Governance Structures— also include the IA activity's relationship with the organization that it supports and the internal and external environments.

Processes, referred to as key process areas (KPAs) in the IA-CM, relate to the six elements and can be found within each capability level. The dark gray in **exhibit I.3** identifies the elements where the IA activity may have more opportunity to independently create and institutionalize the KPAs, up to and including those found in Level 3 – Integrated. Summary descriptions of the elements are found in **exhibit I.4**.

Exhibit I.3:
Elements of Internal Auditing

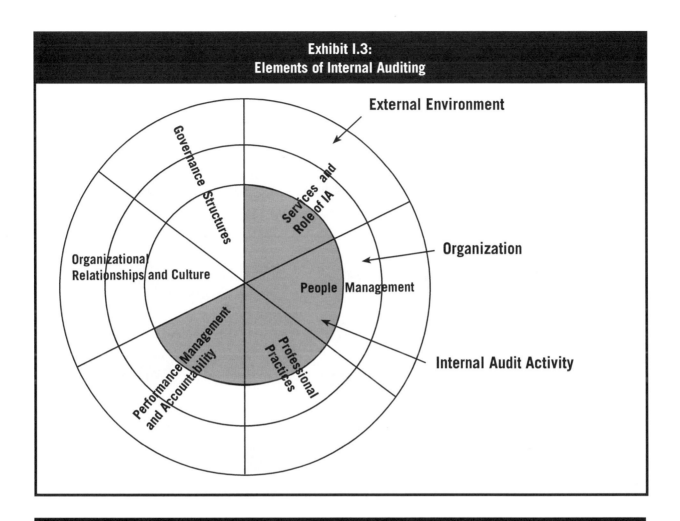

Exhibit I.4:
Descriptions of the Elements of Internal Auditing

Services and Role of Internal Auditing	The role—to provide independent and objective assessments to assist the organization in accomplishing its objectives and improve operations—is found to some degree in most IA activities in the public sector,
	The means or services provided can and do vary among different jurisdictions and environments.
	Services provided are typically based on the organization's needs and the IA activity's authority, scope, and capacity.
	Services include the provision of assurance and advice/consulting and can consist of audits of transactions, compliance, systems, processes, operations, performance/value-for-money, information and related technology, and financial statements and systems.
	Services can also include the capability to assess and advise on organizational governance, risk management strategies/practices, and control processes.
	Services can be performed by the IA activity itself, co-sourced with external service providers, or outsourced.

Exhibit I.4: (continued) **Descriptions of the Elements of Internal Auditing**	
People Management	The process of creating a work environment that enables people to perform to the best of their abilities. The process begins when a job is defined as needed. People management includes: • Identifying specific attributes and developing clear job descriptions. • Recruiting appropriate people through an appropriate selection process. • Identifying job requirements and work objectives based on performance standards, outcomes, and measures. • Providing effective orientation, continuing education, professional development, and training. • Providing ongoing coaching and continuous feedback. • Designing effective compensation and recognition systems. • Providing appropriate promotional and career development opportunities.
Professional Practices	Reflects the full backdrop of policies, processes, and practices that enables the IA activity to be performed effectively and with proficiency and due professional care. Includes the development and use of innovative and evolving frameworks/policies and their application to internal audit programs and operations. Refers to the capacity of the IA activity to align itself with the organization's priorities and risk management strategies and contribute to continuous improvement of the IA activity and the organization. Includes the development and maintenance of a quality assurance and improvement program that covers all aspects of the IA activity.
Performance Management and Accountability	Refers to the information needed to manage, conduct, and control the operations of the IA activity and account for its performance and results. Refers to the identification and communication of sufficient and relevant information to enable people to perform their assigned responsibilities. Includes the development and management of relevant information systems and financial and non-financial (operational and program) performance information. Includes the procedures to manage and protect the integrity of data and to produce and present the appropriate information and results when needed. Refers to reporting to relevant stakeholders and the public on the effectiveness of the IA activity and its value contribution to the organization.

Exhibit I.4: (continued) Descriptions of the Elements of Internal Auditing	
Organizational Relationships and Culture	Refers to the organizational structure and the internal management and relationships within the IA activity itself.
	Includes the CAE's relationships with senior management, and as part of the management team, as well as the ability to advise and influence top-level management and develop effective and ongoing relationships.
	Refers to the IA activity's relationships with other units in the organization, both within the administrative infrastructure and as part of the management regime.
	Includes how the organization's policies, processes, and practices are interpreted and may impact on the IA activity's capacity to access the information and people needed in the conduct of its work.
	Refers to the internal relationships and the organization's internal culture and environment, and how these relationships and the organizational culture may impact on key stakeholders and others outside the organization, including the public.
	Refers to the IA activity's position in the Three Lines of Defense model and its relationship with the first and second lines of defense.
	Refers to relationships with other review groups, including the external auditor or the legislative auditor, if applicable.
Governance Structures	Includes the reporting relationship (administrative and functional) of the CAE, and how the IA activity fits within the organizational and governance structure of the entity.
	Includes the means by which the independence and objectivity of the IA activity is assured; for example, through its mandate, legislated authority, and/or oversight body such as an audit committee.
	Refers to the policies and processes established to provide the necessary authority, support, and resources for the IA activity to carry out its duties and contribute to its effectiveness and independence.

3.2.3 IA-CM One-Page Matrix

Exhibit I.5 presents the IA-CM graphically as a one-page matrix. The vertical axis represents the capability levels—with the capability of the IA activity increasing from bottom to top. The elements of internal auditing are presented on the horizontal axis. The KPAs for each level for each element are identified in the relevant boxes for the appropriate level.

The gray scale on the IA-CM one-page matrix depict the extent or influence that the IA activity has over the elements. Specifically, moving from left to right, the ability of the IA activity itself to independently create and institutionalize the KPAs decreases. For example, the IA activity will likely have greater control over its role and services than over its governance structure. Similarly, the IA activity has potentially less ability to independently institutionalize the KPAs as the capability levels move upward on the matrix from Levels 2 to 5. This shift occurs because the organization and the environment will tend to increase their influence over whether the IA activity is able to institutionalize the KPAs at the higher capability levels.

Furthermore, to move from Level 1 to Level 2 requires certain prerequisites in the environment, such as maturing governance structures and financial management, control, and accountability frameworks, along with government stability, a receptive organizational culture, and central drivers for internal auditing.

In summary, the IA activity will likely have more control in creating and institutionalizing the KPAs found in the elements and levels that are dark gray.

	Exhibit I.5: **Internal Audit Capability Model Matrix**					
	Services and Role of IA	**People Management**	**Professional Practices**	**Performance Management and Accountability**	**Organizational Relationships and Culture**	**Governance Structures**
Level 5 – Optimizing	IA Recognized as Key Agent of Change	Leadership Involvement with Professional Bodies Workforce Projection	Continuous Improvement in Professional Practices Strategic IA Planning	Outcome Performance and Value to Organization Achieved	Effective and Ongoing Relationships	Independence, Power, and Authority of the IA Activity
Level 4 – Managed	Overall Assurance on Governance, Risk Management, and Control	IA Contributes to Management Development IA Activity Supports Professional Bodies Workforce Planning	Audit Strategy Leverages Organization's Management of Risk	Integration of Qualitative and Quantitative Performance Measures	CAE Advises and Influences Top-Level Management	Independent Oversight of the IA Activity
Level 3 – Integrated	Advisory Services Performance/ Value-for-Money Audits	Team Building and Competency Professionally Qualified Staff Workforce Coordination	Quality Management Framework Risk-Based Audit Plans	Performance Measures Cost Information IA Management Reports	Coordination with Other Review Groups Integral Component of Management Team	CAE Reports to Top-Level Authority Management Oversight and Support of the IA Activity Funding Mechanisms
Level 2 – Infrastructure	Compliance Auditing	Individual Professional Development Skilled People Identified and Recruited	Professional Practices and Processes Framework Audit Plan Based on Management/ Stakeholder Priorities	IA Operating Budget IA Business Plan	Managing within the IA Activity	Full Access to the Organization's Information, Assets, and People Reporting Relationships Established
Level 1 – Initial	Ad hoc and unstructured; isolated single audits or reviews of documents and transactions for accuracy and compliance; outputs dependent upon the skills of specific individuals holding the position; no specific professional practices established other than those provided by professional associations; funding approved by management, as needed; absence of infrastructure; auditors likely part of a larger organizational unit; no established capabilities; therefore, no specific key process areas					

3.2.4 What is a Key Process Area (KPA)?

Each capability level consists of one or more descriptors of what it means to achieve that level, which are called KPAs. These are associated with the six elements of internal auditing.

KPAs are the main building blocks that determine the capability of an IA activity. They identify what must be in place and sustained at a given capability level before the IA activity can advance to the next capability level in a particular element. However, it is only when an IA activity has institutionalized all of the KPAs associated with a given level of internal audit capability for all elements that it may be considered to have achieved that level. In other words, all of the KPAs in each element up to and including that level must be mastered and institutionalized into the culture of the IA activity for internal audit to fully achieve a particular level.

> **KPAs identify what must be in place and sustained.**

By definition, KPAs are expressed within an element at a single capability level. There are, however, relationships among the KPAs that stretch across the elements and through the capability levels.

Each KPA consists of a purpose, essential activities, outputs, outcomes, and institutionalizing practices.

Purpose: The purpose of a KPA summarizes the intended outcome or state that must exist for that KPA. The state must be implemented in an effective and lasting way. The extent to which the purpose has been accomplished is an indicator of how much capability the IA activity has established at that capability level. The purpose signifies the scope and intent of each KPA.

Essential Activities: Each KPA identifies a group of related activities that, when performed collectively, achieve the purpose. In turn, these activities produce outputs and outcomes.

Outputs and Outcomes: Certain immediate outputs and mid to longer-term outcomes are associated with every KPA. For the purposes of the IA-CM, outputs relate to "what is done" and outcomes relate to "what difference transpired" and the value that it has added to the organization and its stakeholders. Outputs are typically identified as the accomplishment or product of the essential activities. The assumption is that the activities need to be delivered as intended before the expected outcomes can occur.

Institutionalizing Practices: Certain practices must be mastered and institutionalized into the IA activity to achieve a particular KPA. The model is not intended to be prescriptive in terms of how a process should be carried out, but rather what should be done. Institutionalizing practices for a particular IA activity will vary depending on the external environment, the organization's nature and complexity, and the attributes of the IA activity. For illustrative purposes and clarity, some examples of institutionalizing practices are provided for each KPA. The examples identify various ways of implementing the KPA, but they are not intended to be prescriptive or exhaustive. Furthermore, the institutionalizing practice examples are not intended to be necessarily unique to a particular KPA, but rather may demonstrate degrees of sophistication representing the achievement of the essential activities for different KPAs at different levels.

3.2.5 Achieving a Capability Level

Achieving a given capability level involves mastering all of the KPAs found in the elements included in that level and ensuring that these KPAs are institutionalized within the IA activity. Institutionalizing KPAs at one level establishes the basis for practices and capabilities at the next level.

Mastering KPAs: As noted in **exhibit I.6**, once an IA activity has done the necessary work to realize the outputs and outcomes associated with a KPA, it has mastered that KPA.

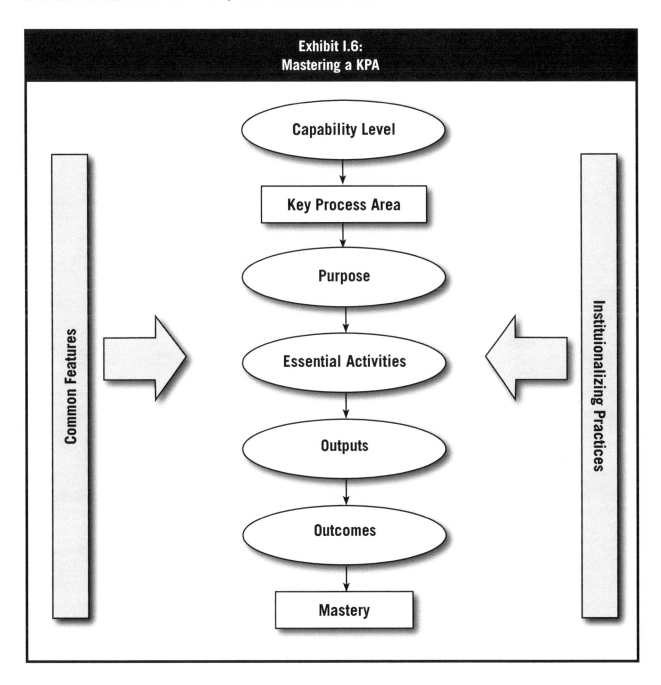

Institutionalizing KPAs: In addition to mastering the KPA, the IA activity must institutionalize the KPA by incorporating the essential activities associated with it into the culture of the IA activity. In this way, the KPA will be sustainable and repeatable and become a basic building block that contributes to reaching a particular capability level.

Common Features: Institutionalizing a KPA requires that certain common features, which describe the activities and infrastructure supportive of institutionalization, are present. The five types of common features include: commitment to perform, ability to perform, activities performed, measurement, and verification.

3.2.6 Common Features

Exhibit I.7 identifies the five types of common features: commitment to perform, ability to perform, activities performed, measurement, and verification. They describe means to institutionalize and ensure the sustainability of the KPA.

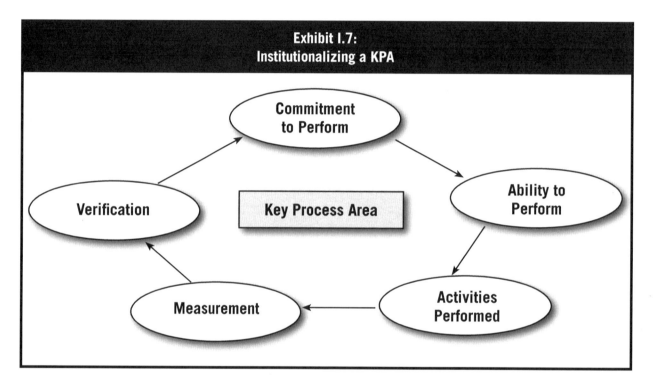

Exhibit I.7:
Institutionalizing a KPA

Commitment to perform is the commitment to master the KPAs associated with reaching a particular capability level. It can include developing *policies*—policy statements generally refer to establishing, maintaining, and following a documented organizational policy for supporting the essential activities of a particular KPA. This emphasizes the importance of organizational commitment. Also included in this common feature is *sponsorship* through support by senior management. Clearly, senior management support is an important element in developing strong internal audit capabilities.

Ability to perform relates to the ability to carry out the essential **activities** competently. It could reflect the need for appropriate *resources* (for example, human resources, dollars, time, and access to specialized skills and appropriate tools, including technology-based tools). It may also address having a *plan* in place to carry out the activity, assigning *responsibility* to carry out the plan, and providing appropriate *training and development*.

Examples of common features relating to "commitment to perform" and "ability to perform" are provided as "Institutionalizing Practice Examples" for each KPA.

The **activities performed** feature describes implementation activities. Because the activities performed are specific to a KPA, the IA-CM identifies them separately for each KPA as "essential activities."

The key practices undertaken for the common features of measurement and verification are generally the same for each KPA. For example, **measurement** refers to *ongoing measurement and analysis* of activities and progress in achieving the KPA's purpose. **Verification** includes *continuous verification* to ensure that activities have been carried out in accordance with established policies and procedures. This could include independent review, management review, or senior management oversight.

Through the presence of such common features, a climate is provided that contributes to and supports a foundation for reaching an internal audit capability level appropriate to the organization.

3.3 KPAs by Internal Audit Element

KPAs at each level in each element build upon one another and establish the foundation for implementing a KPA at a higher level. For example, in the element Services and Role of Internal Auditing, once the IA activity has institutionalized Compliance Auditing, that KPA will continue to be performed even as other KPAs at higher capability levels (Performance/Value-for-Money Audits and Advisory Services) are also performed.

Exhibit I.8 identifies the purposes for each KPA in each element by level to demonstrate the relationships among the KPAs in each element and how they build upon one another as the capability of internal auditing increases from Level 1 – Initial to Level 5 – Optimizing. Additional details of each KPA, including the essential activities, outputs, outcomes, and institutionalizing practice examples, are found in the Application Guide.

Exhibit I.8: Purposes of KPAs by Internal Audit Element	
Services and Role of Internal Auditing	
5 – Optimizing	**Internal Audit Recognized as Key Agent of Change** **Purpose** To have sufficiently developed the professional and leadership capacity of the IA activity to provide foresight and serve as a catalyst to achieve positive change in the organization.
4 – Managed	**Overall Assurance on Governance, Risk Management, and Control** **Purpose** To conduct sufficient work to provide an opinion on the overall adequacy and effectiveness of the organization's governance, risk management, and control processes. The IA activity has coordinated its audit services to be sufficiently comprehensive that it can provide reasonable assurance at a corporate level that these processes are adequate and functioning as intended to meet the organization's objectives.

Exhibit I.8: (continued) **Purposes of KPAs by Internal Audit Element**	
3 – Integrated	**Advisory Services** **Purpose** To analyze a situation and/or provide guidance and advice to management. Advisory services add value without the internal auditor assuming management responsibility. Advisory services are those that are directed toward facilitation rather than assurance and include training, systems development reviews, performance and control self-assessment, counseling, and advice. **Performance/Value-for-Money Audits** **Purpose** To assess and report on the efficiency, effectiveness, and economy of operations, activities, or programs; or conduct engagements on governance, risk management, and control. Performance/value-for-money auditing covers the full spectrum of operating and business processes, the associated management controls, and the results achieved.
2 – Infrastructure	**Compliance Auditing** **Purpose** To carry out an audit of conformity and adherence of a particular area, process, or system to policies, plans, procedures, laws, regulations, contracts, or other requirements that govern the conduct of the area, process, or system subject to audit.
1 – Initial	**No KPAs** Isolated single audits or reviews of documents and transactions for accuracy and compliance.
People Management	
5 – Optimizing	**Leadership Involvement with Professional Bodies** **Purpose** To facilitate and support top leaders of the IA activity becoming key leaders within relevant professional bodies. In addition to making contributions to the profession through their volunteer work, the CAE and other internal auditors will become thought leaders and influence the growth and evolution of the profession. Participating in the administration and/or leadership of professional bodies helps auditors learn and practice higher-level people skills, since their roles vis-à-vis their colleagues require different means of interacting from their "auditor" or "manager" role within their own organization. **Workforce Projection** **Purpose** To coordinate long-term workforce development activities to meet future business needs of the IA activity. Workforce projection involves developing a strategic workforce plan that sets out the IA activity's objectives for competency development and workforce activities in conjunction with the organization's projected strategic needs, and developing plans to guide workforce development activities for the IA activity.

Exhibit I.8: (continued) **Purposes of KPAs by Internal Audit Element**	
4 – Managed	**Internal Audit Contributes to Management Development** **Purpose** To integrate the development of the organization's managers with the training and experiences of the IA activity and vice versa. The organization and the IA activity pursue a strategy to encourage people with a good understanding of governance, risk management, and controls to work and contribute throughout the organization. **IA Activity Supports Professional Bodies** **Purpose** To provide leadership and professional development opportunities for the internal audit staff by supporting their involvement and participation in professional bodies. **Workforce Planning** **Purpose** To coordinate workforce activities to achieve current business needs of the IA activity. Workforce planning involves developing a workforce plan that sets out the resources, skills, training, and tools required to conduct the audits that have been identified (or are proposed) in the periodic audit and services plan.
3 – Integrated	**Team Building and Competency** **Purpose** To develop staff members' capacity to function effectively in a team environment, beginning with focus on the individual project team. Because many public sector audits cover scopes that require the concerted effort of a team of auditors to conduct, and because the skills needed to conduct an audit are not necessarily the same skills to work effectively in a group environment, additional team competencies are required. **Professionally Qualified Staff** **Purpose** To staff the IA activity with professionally qualified staff and retain the individuals who have demonstrated a minimum level of competence. **Workforce Coordination** **Purpose** To coordinate the development of the periodic audit and services plan to the human resource levels authorized to the IA activity. Because resources are often constrained, the IA activity needs to use appropriate methods to set priorities on planned projects and services to limit its commitments to a "doable" quantity and type of projects and services.

Exhibit I.8: (continued) **Purposes of KPAs by Internal Audit Element**	
2 – Infrastructure	**Individual Professional Development** **Purpose** To ensure that internal auditors continuously maintain and enhance their professional capabilities. **Skilled People Identified and Recruited** **Purpose** To identify and attract people with the necessary competencies and relevant skills to carry out the work of the IA activity. Appropriately qualified and recruited internal auditors are more likely to provide credibility to the internal audit results.
1 – Initial	**No KPAs** Outputs are dependent upon the skills of specific individuals holding the position.
Professional Practices	
5 – Optimizing	**Continuous Improvement in Professional Practices** **Purpose** To integrate the performance data, global leading practices, and feedback received from ongoing quality assurance and improvement program processes to continuously strengthen and develop the IA activity's capacity to deliver world-class internal auditing. **Strategic Internal Audit Planning** **Purpose** To understand the organization's strategic directions and emerging issues and risks, and change the IA activity's skillsets and audit services to meet potential future needs.
4 – Managed	**Audit Strategy Leverages Organization's Management of Risk** **Purpose** To link the IA activity's periodic audit and services plan with the organization's enterprise risk management strategies and practices.
3 – Integrated	**Quality Management Framework** **Purpose** To establish and maintain processes to continuously monitor, assess, and improve the effectiveness of the IA activity. Processes include ongoing internal monitoring of the performance of the IA activity as well as periodic internal and external quality assessments. **Risk-Based Audit Plans** **Purpose** To systematically assess risks and focus the priorities of the IA activity's periodic audit and services plan on risk exposures throughout the organization.

Exhibit I.8: (continued) **Purposes of KPAs by Internal Audit Element**	
2 – Infrastructure	**Professional Practices and Processes Framework** **Purpose** To help facilitate the performance of audit engagements with the independence and objectivity, and proficiency and due professional care envisaged in the internal audit charter and the Mission of Internal Audit, the Definition of Internal Auditing, the Code of Ethics, the *Core Principles,* and the *Standards*. The professional practices and processes framework includes the policies, processes, and procedures that will guide the IA activity in managing its operations; developing its internal audit work program; and planning, performing, and reporting on the results of internal audits. **Audit Plan Based on Management/Stakeholder Priorities** **Purpose** To develop periodic (annual or multiyear) plans for which audits and/or other services will be provided, based on consultations with management and/or other stakeholders.
1 – Initial	**No KPAs** No specific professional practices established other than those provided by professional associations.
Performance Management and Accountability	
5 – Optimizing	**Outcome Performance and Value to the Organization Achieved** **Purpose** To report on the effectiveness of the IA activity to demonstrate transparency and accountability to the organization's stakeholders and the public, and identify the contribution and impact made by the IA activity with the resources provided.
4 – Managed	**Integration of Qualitative and Quantitative Performance Measures** **Purpose** To enable the IA activity to use information on performance to measure and monitor fluctuations that affect its results. The activity has balanced its use of quantitative and qualitative data to help it achieve its strategic objectives.
3 – Integrated	**Performance Measures** **Purpose** In addition to cost data, to develop meaningful indicators and measures that enable the IA activity to measure and report on its performance and routinely monitor its progress against targets to ensure that results are achieved as economically and efficiently as possible. These will be primarily process and input measures, and some output or qualitative outcome measures.

Exhibit I.8: (continued) **Purposes of KPAs by Internal Audit Element**	
3 – Integrated (continued)	**Cost Information** **Purpose** To provide sufficient information from the financial tracking system so that the IA activity understands the cost information sufficiently to use it to manage its services as economically and efficiently as possible. This practice goes slightly beyond budget variances and integrates the relationship of outputs to inputs. **Internal Audit Management Reports** **Purpose** To receive and use information to manage the IA activity's day-to-day operations, support decision-making, and demonstrate accountability.
2 – Infrastructure	**Internal Audit Operating Budget** **Purpose** To be allocated and use its own operating budget to plan the services of the IA activity. **Internal Audit Business Plan** **Purpose** To establish a periodic plan for delivering the services of the IA activity, including administrative and support services, and the expected results.
1 – Initial	**No KPAs** Ad hoc and unstructured; funding approved by management, as needed.
Organizational Relationships and Culture	
5 – Optimizing	**Effective and Ongoing Relationships** **Purpose** To use strong relationship management skills of the CAE for maintaining appropriate visibility and alignment with key stakeholders, management, and audit committee needs and expectations.
4 – Managed	**CAE Advises and Influences Top-Level Management** **Purpose** To facilitate the organization's understanding and appreciation of the vision, leadership, and foresight of the CAE, and to develop a professional relationship with top-level management that fosters frank exchanges, while maintaining independence and objectivity. Senior management values the CAE for advice on strategic issues.
3 – Integrated	**Coordination with Other Review Groups** **Purpose** To share information and coordinate activities with other internal and external providers of assurance and advisory services to ensure appropriate organizational coverage and minimize duplication of effort. **Integral Component of Management Team** **Purpose** To participate in the organization's management activities in some form as a valued member of the management team. Although the CAE does not carry out management's responsibilities, the CAE is included in communications and forums of the management team, and as an observer, is able to maintain a channel of communication with senior management.

	Exhibit I.8: (continued) Purposes of KPAs by Internal Audit Element	
2 – Infrastructure	**Managing within the IA Activity** **Purpose** To focus the management effort of the IA activity on its own operations and relationships within the activity itself, such as organizational structure, people management, budget preparation and monitoring, annual planning, providing the necessary audit tools and technology, and performing audits. Interactions with organizational managers are focused on carrying out the business of the IA activity.
1 – Initial	**No KPAs** Absence of IA activity infrastructure.
Governance Structures	
5 – Optimizing	**Independence, Power, and Authority of the IA Activity** **Purpose** To fully actualize the IA activity's independence, power, and authority.
4 – Managed	**Independent Oversight of the IA Activity** **Purpose** To establish an oversight body, including members independent of the organization's management, to assure the independence of the IA activity, broaden the activity's scope of input and influence, and help strengthen the organization's accountability.
3 – Integrated	**CAE Reports to Top-Level Authority** **Purpose** To strengthen the CAE's independence by establishing a direct functional reporting relationship to the governing body and a direct administrative reporting relationship to either the CEO or governing body. **Management Oversight and Support of the IA Activity** **Purpose** To establish a mechanism/process within the organization to provide oversight and advice to the IA activity, review its results, and ensure appropriate actions are taken to strengthen its independence. Operating managers respect audit independence, are responsive to audit requests, and provide constructive feedback to facilitate the audit process. Involvement of a variety of managers in the decisions related to the IA activity helps to extend the activity's support and scope beyond a single individual and helps ensure its independence. **Funding Mechanisms** **Purpose** To establish a robust and transparent funding process that ensures adequate resources to allow the IA activity to discharge its obligations.

Exhibit I.8: (continued) **Purposes of KPAs by Internal Audit Element**	
2 – Infrastructure	**Full Access to the Organization's Information, Assets, and People** **Purpose** To provide the authority for the IA activity to obtain access to all the information, assets, and people that it requires to carry out its duties. **Reporting Relationships Established** **Purpose** To establish formal reporting relationships (administrative and functional) for the IA activity.
1 – Initial	**No KPAs** Auditors are likely part of a larger organizational unit.

4. Selected Bibliography

1. *A New Order: The Key Skillsets Necessary to Thrive as Head of Internal Audit* (Thomson Reuters, June 2015).

2. Abela, Carman, and James R. Mitchell, *Unlocking the Power of Internal Audit in the Public Sector* (The Institute of Internal Auditors Canada, 2014).

3. *Arriving at Internal Audit's Tipping Point Amid Business Transformation*, 2016 Internal Audit Capabilities and Needs Survey Report (Protiviti, 2016).

4. Committee of Sponsoring Organizations of the Treadway Commission (COSO) 2013 *Internal Control - Integrated Framework*.

5. *COMPENDIUM of the public internal control systems in the EU Member States 2014*, Second Edition, European Commission.

6. *Evolution or irrelevance? Internal Audit at a crossroads*, Deloitte's Global Chief Audit Executive Survey, 2016.

7. *Global Pulse of Internal Audit, Embracing Opportunities in a Dynamic Environment*, Audit Executive Center (Lake Mary, FL: The Institute of Internal Auditors, July 2015).

8. Haron, H., and T. C. Qun, "The Relationship between Internal Audit Characteristic, Audit Committee Characteristic and Interaction between Internal Audit and Audit Committee on Internal Audit Contribution," *The Advocate*, June 2016, Malaysian Institute of Corporate Governance.

9. Haron, Hasnah, Ishak Ismail, Yuaraj Ganesan, Fathyah Hashim, and Aireen Mak Siew Fern, "Assessment on Internal Audit Capability Level in a Public Sector Organisation," Keeping in Touch, The Institute of Internal Auditors Malaysia, Issue 02/2016, April – June 2016.

10. *HM Treasury: The effectiveness of internal audit in central government*, National Audit Office, June 2012.

11. IIA Position Paper "The Three Lines of Defense in Effective Risk Management and Control" (Lake Mary, FL: The Institute of Internal Auditors, January 2013).

12. IIA Practice Guide "Chief Audit Executives Appointment, Performance Evaluation, and Termination" (Lake Mary, FL: The Institute of Internal Auditors, 2010).

13. IIA Practice Guide "Creating an Internal Audit Competency Process for the Public Sector" (Lake Mary, FL: The Institute of Internal Auditors, February 2015).

14. IIA Practice Guide "Developing the Internal Audit Strategic Plan" (Lake Mary, FL: The Institute of Internal Auditors, July 2012.

15. IIA Practice Guide "Internal Audit and the Second Line of Defense" (Lake Mary, FL: The Institute of Internal Auditors, January 2016).

16. IIA Practice Guide "Measuring Internal Audit Effectiveness and Efficiency" (Lake Mary, FL: The Institute of Internal Auditors, December 2010).

17. IIA Practice Guide "Quality Assurance and Improvement Program" (Lake Mary, FL: The Institute of Internal Auditors, March 2012).

18. IIA Practice Guide "Reliance by Internal Audit on Other Assurance Providers" (Lake Mary, FL: The Institute of Internal Auditors, December 2011).

19. IIA Practice Guide "Selecting, Using, and Creating Maturity Models: A Tool for Assurance and Consulting Engagements" (Lake Mary, FL: The Institute of Internal Auditors, July 2013). (Presentation on Process Maturity Model: A Tool for Internal Auditors, The IIA).

20. IIA Practice Guide "Talent Management: Recruiting, Developing, Motivating, and Retaining Great Team Members" (Lake Mary, FL: The Institute of Internal Auditors, December 2015).

21. *Implementing a New Internal Audit Function in the Public Sector*, Supplemental Guidance, April 2012.

22. *Independent Audit Committees in Public Sector Organizations*, Global Public Sector Insight, June 2014.

23. *Internal Audit Ambition Model* (The Institute of Internal Auditors Netherlands, June 2016).

24. *Internal audit customer handbook*, HM Treasury, July 2013.

25. *Internal Audit - Driving for Success: Navigating the Basics of Internal Audit* (Thomson Reuters, 2016).

26. *Internal Audit Maturity Assessment* (The Institute of Internal Auditors, Australia, 2014).

27. *Internal Audit Quality Assessment Framework*, HM Treasury, September 2011.

28. *Leveraging COSO Across the Three Lines of Defense* (The Institute of Internal Auditors and COSO, July 2015).

29. MacRae, Elizabeth, "Improving the Effectiveness of the IG at the Ministry of Public Works (The IA-CM takes a "building block" approach to establishing internal auditing)." *Prakarsa Journal of Indonesian Infrastructure Initiative*, Issue 13/January 2013.

30. MacRae, Elizabeth, and Diane Van Gils, *Internal Audit Capabilities and Performance Levels in the Public Sector*, A Global Assessment Based on The IIA's 2010 Global Internal Audit Survey and The IIA's Internal Audit Capability Model for the Public Sector (Lake Mary, FL: The Institute of Internal Auditors Research Foundation, 2014).

31. Mermod, Aslı Yüksel, and Gökhan Sungun, "INTERNAL AUDIT POSITIONING - FOUR STAGE MODEL," *Journal of Business, Economics & Finance*, 2013, Volume 2 Issue 1, 65–89.

32. *Moving Up the Internal Audit Maturity Curve Model* (Thomson Reuters, 2015).

33. *Public Sector Internal Audit, An Investment in Assurance and Business Improvement*, Better Practice Guide (Australian National Audit Office, September 2012).

34. *Pulse of the Profession, Enhancing Value Through Collaboration: A Call to Action*, Audit Executive Center (Lake Mary, FL: The Institute of Internal Auditors, July 2014).

35. Software Engineering Institute, Capability Maturity Model Integration (CMMI®), Version 1.1, Carnegie Mellon University, March 2002.

36. Software Engineering Institute, CMMI® for Development, Version 1.2, Carnegie Mellon University, March 2006.

37. Software Engineering Institute, People Capability Maturity Model (P-CMM®), Version 2.0, Carnegie Mellon University, July 2001.

38. Software Engineering Institute, Product Development Capability Maturity Model (PD-CMM®), Version 1.0, Carnegie Mellon University, 2000.

39. Software Engineering Institute, Software Capability Maturity Model (SM-CMM®), Version 1.0 (1991), Version 1.1 (1993), Version 2 (1998), Carnegie Mellon University.

40. Software Engineering Institute, Systems Engineering Capability Maturity Model (SE-CMM®), Version 1.1, Carnegie Mellon University, 1995.

41. Sondh, Puneet, "Insights from the Study of Internal Audit Evolution in Selected ASEAN Central Banks," February 2017, Development Asia Initiative of the Asian Development Bank.

42. *The Framework for Internal Audit Effectiveness: The New IPPF* (Lake Mary, FL: The Institute of Internal Auditors, 2015).

43. *The IIA Global Internal Audit Competency Framework* (Lake Mary, FL: The Institute of Internal Auditors, 2013).

44. *The Role of Auditing in Public Sector Governance*, Supplemental Guidance, 2nd Edition (Lake Mary, FL: The Institute of Internal Auditors, January 2012).

45. *Value Proposition of Internal Auditing and the Internal Audit Capability Model*, Supplemental Guidance (Lake Mary, FL: The Institute of Internal Auditors, March 2012).

46. Van Rensburg, Jacobus Oosthuizen Janse, and Philna Coetzee, "Internal audit public sector capability: a case study." *Journal of Public Affairs*, Volume 16 Number 2, 181–191, 19 June 2015 in Wiley Online Library.

CBOK Reports

1. Abdolmohammadi, Mohammad, Giuseppe D'Onza, and Gerrit Sarens, *Benchmarking Internal Audit Maturity: A High-Level Look at Audit Planning and Processes Worldwide* (Lake Mary, FL: The Institute of Internal Auditors Research Foundation, 2016).

2. Araj, Farah, G., *Responding to Fraud Risk: Exploring Where Internal Auditing Stands* (Lake Mary, FL: The Institute of Internal Auditors Research Foundation, 2016).

3. Barr-Pulliam, Derek, *Engaging Third Parties for Internal Audit Activities: Strategies for Successful Relationships* (Lake Mary, FL: The Institute of Internal Auditors Research Foundation, 2016).

4. Burke, Jennifer F., and Steven E. Jameson, *A Global View of Financial Services Auditing: Challenges, Opportunities, and the Future* (Lake Mary, FL: The Institute of Internal Auditors Research Foundation, 2016).

5. Cangemi, Michael P., *Staying a Step Ahead: Internal Audit's Use of Technology* (Lake Mary, FL: The Institute of Internal Auditors Research Foundation, 2016).

6. Flora, Philip E., and Sajay Rai, *Navigating Technology's Top 10 Risks: Internal Audit's Role* (Lake Mary, FL: The Institute of Internal Auditors Research Foundation, 2016).

7. Harrington, Larry and Arthur Piper, *Driving Success in a Changing World: 10 Imperatives for Internal Audit* (Lake Mary, FL: The Institute of Internal Auditors Research Foundation, 2016).

8. Huibers, Sam, C. J., *Combined Assurance: One Language, One Voice, One View* (Lake Mary, FL: The Institute of Internal Auditors Research Foundation, 2016).

9. Iyer, Venkataraman, *CAE Career Paths: Characteristics and Competencies of Today's Internal Audit Leaders* (Lake Mary, FL: The Institute of Internal Auditors Research Foundation, 2016).

10. Piper, Arthur, *Auditing the Public Sector: Managing Expectations, Delivering Results* (Lake Mary, FL: The Institute of Internal Auditors Research Foundation, 2016).

11. Rittenberg, Larry E., *Interacting with Audit Committees: The Way Forward for Internal Audit* (Lake Mary, FL: The Institute of Internal Auditors Research Foundation, 2016).

12. Rose, James, *Mapping Your Career: Competencies Necessary for Internal Audit Excellence* (Lake Mary, FL: The Institute of Internal Auditors Research Foundation, 2016).

13. Rose, James, *Top 7 Skills CAEs Want: Building the Right Mix of Talent for Your Organization* (Lake Mary, FL: The Institute of Internal Auditors Research Foundation, 2016).

14. Seago, Jane, *Delivering on the Promise: Measuring Internal Audit Value and Performance* (Lake Mary, FL: The Institute of Internal Auditors Research Foundation, 2016).

15. Sobel, Paul J., *Who Owns Risk? A Look at Internal Audit's Changing Role* (Lake Mary, FL: The Institute of Internal Auditors Research Foundation, 2016).

16. Tsintzas, Eleftherios, *Lifelong Learning for Internal Auditors: Certification and Training Levels Worldwide* (Lake Mary, FL: The Institute of Internal Auditors Research Foundation, 2016).

17. Turner, Bruce, *Ways to Motivate Your Staff: Shaping an Audit Team that Adds Value and Inspires Business Improvement* (Lake Mary, FL: The Institute of Internal Auditors Research Foundation, 2016).

18. The IIA - https://theiia.org

Annex A: Original Research Purpose, Methodology, and Onsite Validations

A.1 Research Purpose and Methodology

The ultimate purpose of the original research project was to develop an IA-CM to use globally as a basis for implementing and institutionalizing effective internal auditing in the public sector. The primary lines of enquiry were intended to explore and identify:

- The overall characteristics at each capability level for the IA activity and the organization that it supports.

- The elements that make up the IA activity and the key process areas at each capability level and within each element.

- The activities and practices of each key process area that need to function effectively and the corresponding purpose that needs to be achieved to move to the next level.

The project was composed of two phases. The first phase took place from October 2006 to April 2007 and the second from November 2007 to May 2009.

Phase 1 identified the characteristics at each level, the elements of the IA activity, and the key process areas (KPAs) at each level and for each element. An extensive literature and documentation review was conducted along with input through focus groups and workshops from over 50 internal audit professionals from over 20 countries.

Phase 2 built on the results of Phase 1 by refining and elaborating on the five levels of capability, further distinguishing them, and evaluating aspects of each level that contributed to the capability for implementing the next level. The essential activities, outputs, outcomes, and means to institutionalize the KPAs were developed.

Phase 2 confirmed the appropriateness of each level and the KPAs within the internal audit elements by:

- Identifying real-life IA activities that exemplified each level, and comparing across the elements to ensure that the examples were truly representative of the model; and

- Validating, through extensive interaction and communication with IA activities world-wide, that the essential activities, outputs, and outcomes identified in the KPAs within each element at each level constituted the basis and provided the capability for functioning effectively, and that they established the foundational (or systemic) capacity to move on to the next level.

The research team felt that global validation was critical to the usability and acceptance of the model. The Internal Auditing Department of the World Bank worked with the Foundation to ensure sufficient global validation—considering different forms of government, stages of government's maturity, and cultures of countries and continents. A detailed validation plan was developed to identify public sector IA activities at each of the capability levels at different locations around the world.

Extensive consultation and interaction took place with internal audit professionals, key stakeholders, and communities of interest, including senior management, audit committee members, and Supreme Audit Institutions as well as relevant service providers. The model was validated and refined to ensure that it was useable, useful, practical, and relevant for public sector IA activities.

A detailed report on the results of each onsite validation (which included evolving/best-practice examples, suggestions for improving the IA activity, and refinements to the IA-CM) was provided to validation participants. Some of the evolving and best-practice examples were highlighted in the original IA-CM Research Report published in 2009.

Sixteen IA activities in public sector environments worldwide participated in onsite IA-CM validation sessions. Presentations and workshops were also held to obtain additional input. More than 300 people from over 30 countries were consulted during Phase 2. In addition, input was sought from various local internal audit institutes and The IIA's international committees, particularly the PSC.

A.2 Onsite Validations

This section summarizes the IA-CM validation activity undertaken during Phase 2 of the research project—from November 2007 to November 2008. **Exhibit A.1** identifies the IA-CM validations conducted with IA activities worldwide and includes details relating to the internal audit professionals, stakeholders, and others who participated. **Exhibit A.2** describes other global input obtained through interviews, presentations, and focus groups with internal audit professionals and key stakeholders. In the original IA-CM Application Guide, this section also included highlights of some evolving and best-practice examples noted during the global validations conducted from February to November 2008.

Exhibit A.1: IA-CM Validation Sessions with IA Activities					
Country	**Organization**	**IA Activity**	**IA Professionals**	**Stakeholders**	**Date**
Republic of Croatia	Ministry of Finance	Internal Audit Service	CAE Others	SAI CHU SM WB IIA	February 2008

Exhibit A.1: (continued) IA-CM Validation Sessions with IA Activities					
Country	**Organization**	**IA Activity**	**IA Professionals**	**Stakeholders**	**Date**
Australia	Queensland Department of Education, Training, and the Arts	Internal Audit Unit	CAE Others QAR	IIA	March 2008
United States	Texas State Commission on Environmental Quality	Chief Auditor's Office	CAE Others QAR		April 2008
United States	City of Austin, Texas	Office of the City Auditor	CAE Others		April 2008
Argentina	Department of Defense Agency	Internal Audit Unit	CAE Others	SIGEN SM IIA	May 2008
United States	World Bank Group	Internal Auditing Department	CAE Others		June 2008
Republic of Kenya	Ministry of Finance	Internal Audit Department	Internal Auditor-General CAEs Others	SAI SM WB IIA	July 2008
Republic of Uganda	Ministry of Finance	Internal Audit	Commissioner Assistant Commissioner CAEs Others	SAI SM WB IIA	July 2008

Exhibit A.1: (continued) **IA-CM Validation Sessions with IA Activities**					
Country	**Organization**	**IA Activity**	**IA Professionals**	**Stakeholders**	**Date**
United Republic of Tanzania	Treasury	Internal Audit	Assistant Accountant-General CAEs Others	SAI SM WB IIA Others	July 2008
United Republic of Tanzania	SUMATRA	Performance Audit	CAE Others	SM	July 2008
Arab Republic of Egypt	Ministry of Finance Ministry of Investment	Audit groups	Ministry Officials CAEs Others	WB IIA	August 2008
India	Ministry of Finance, Office of the Controller General of Accounts	Centre of Excellence in IA	Controller General of Accounts, Chief Controller of Accounts CAEs Others	SAI SM WB	Sept. 2008
Malaysia	Ministry of Finance	Accountant General Department	CAEs Others	SAI IIA Others	Sept. 2008
Socialist Republic of Vietnam	Ministry of Finance	Inspection Directorate, Accounting and Auditing Department	Ministry Officials CAE	SAI WB Others	Sept. 2008

	Exhibit A.1: (continued) IA-CM Validation Sessions with IA Activities				
Country	**Organization**	**IA Activity**	**IA Professionals**	**Stakeholders**	**Date**
United Kingdom	National Offender Management Service	Audit and Corporate Assurance	CAE Others QAR	SAI AC SM IIA	October 2008
Belgium	European Commission	Internal Audit Service	CAEs Others QAR	AC SM	October 2008

Key:

AC – Audit Committee Member   QAR – External Assessor
CAE – Chief Audit Executive   SAI – Representatives of the Supreme Audit Institution
CHU – Central Harmonization Unit   SM – Senior Management
IIA – Representatives of the local IIA Institute   WB – Representatives of the World Bank

	Exhibit A.2: Other IA-CM Validation Input		
Country	**Venue**	**Participants**	**Date**
United States	Presentation and Discussion	WB Others	November 2007
Turkey	WB Workshop	19 Countries	February 2008
Australia (Sydney)	SOPAC Focus Group	Public Sector CAEs	March 2008
Australia (Canberra)	Interviews–National Government	CAEs SAI	March 2008
Argentina	Presentation–IIA-Argentina	IIA Members	May 2008
United States	Meeting	GAO, Washington	May 2008
Republic of Kenya	Presentation–IIA-Kenya	IIA Members	July 2008

	Exhibit A.2: (continued) Other IA-CM Validation Input		
Country	**Venue**	**Participants**	**Date**
Republic of Uganda	Interviews–Ministry of Local Government	CAEs and Other IA Professionals	July 2008
Malaysia	Interviews–Public/Private Sector	CAEs Academics	September 2008
France	Discussion Group	CAEs IIA	October 2008
Canada	Presentation–Government Internal Auditors Council of Canada	CAEs—Canada's Provinces and Territories, Assistant Comptroller General, Treasury Board Secretariat	October 2008
Canada	Presentations–Office of the Comptroller General	Federal CAEs and Representatives of the Office of the Comptroller General	November 2008
Key: AC – Audit Committee Member CAE – Chief Audit Executive CHU – Central Harmonization Unit IIA – Representatives of the local IIA Institute		QAR – External Assessor SAI – Representatives of the Supreme Audit Institution SM – Senior Management WB – Representatives of the World Bank	

II. APPLICATION GUIDE—THE IA-CM IN DETAIL

1. Introduction

The Application Guide describes in detail the various components of the IA-CM and provides advice in applying and interpreting the model. It begins by illustrating the IA-CM graphically as a one-page matrix.

Section 2.2 describes the six elements of internal auditing: Services and Role of Internal Auditing, People Management, Professional Practices, Performance Management and Accountability, Organizational Relationships and Culture, and Governance Structures.

Section 2.3 describes each capability level in the IA-CM and identifies the capabilities and relationships among the key process areas (KPAs) within the elements at the specific level. For each capability level, an exhibit is included that highlights the purposes for each KPA within each element at that level. The advantages of staying at a particular level and challenges of moving to the next level are explored.

Section 3 of the Application Guide also describes some underlying principles in applying and interpreting the IA-CM, such as whether Level 3 is sufficient, levels can be skipped, KPAs can be ignored, and whether all elements must be at the same capability level. In addition, a discussion of the IA-CM and its relationship with a quality assurance and improvement program is included.

Section 4 presents the detailed KPAs. Each KPA includes its purpose, essential activities, outputs, and outcomes, and identifies institutionalizing practice examples.

Annex B provides some examples of current uses of the IA-CM by IA activities globally.

2. The IA-CM in Detail

2.1 The IA-CM One-Page Matrix

Exhibit II.1 presents the IA-CM as a one-page summary matrix. The vertical axis represents the capability levels—with the capability of the IA activity increasing from bottom to top. The elements of internal auditing are presented on the horizontal axis. The KPAs for each level for each element are identified in the relevant boxes for the appropriate level.

The gray scale on the IA-CM one-page matrix depicts the extent or influence that the IA activity has over the elements. Specifically, moving from left to right, the ability of the IA activity itself to independently create and institutionalize the KPAs decreases. For example, the IA activity will likely have greater control over its role and services than over its governance structure. Similarly, an IA activity has potentially less ability to independently institutionalize the KPAs as the capability levels move upward on the matrix from Levels 2 to 5. This shift occurs because the organization and the environment will tend to increase their influence over whether the IA activity is able to institutionalize the KPAs at the higher capability levels.

Furthermore, to move from Level 1 to Level 2 requires certain prerequisites in the environment, such as maturing governance structures and financial management, control, and accountability frameworks, along with government stability, a receptive organizational culture, and central drivers for internal auditing.

In summary, the IA activity will likely have more control in creating and institutionalizing the KPAs found in the elements and levels that are dark gray.

	Exhibit II.1: Internal Audit Capability Model Matrix					
	Services and Role of IA	People Management	Professional Practices	Performance Management and Accountability	Organizational Relationships and Culture	Governance Structures
Level 5 – Optimizing	IA Recognized as Key Agent of Change	Leadership Involvement with Professional Bodies Workforce Projection	Continuous Improvement in Professional Practices Strategic IA Planning	Outcome Performance and Value to Organization Achieved	Effective and Ongoing Relationships	Independence, Power, and Authority of the IA Activity
Level 4 – Managed	Overall Assurance on Governance, Risk Management, and Control	IA Contributes to Management Development IA Activity Supports Professional Bodies Workforce Planning	Audit Strategy Leverages Organization's Management of Risk	Integration of Qualitative and Quantitative Performance Measures	CAE Advises and Influences Top-Level Management	Independent Oversight of the IA Activity
Level 3 – Integrated	Advisory Services Performance/ Value-for-Money Audits	Team Building and Competency Professionally Qualified Staff Workforce Coordination	Quality Management Framework Risk-Based Audit Plans	Performance Measures Cost Information IA Management Reports	Coordination with Other Review Groups Integral Component of Management Team	CAE Reports to Top-Level Authority Management Oversight and Support of the IA Activity Funding Mechanisms
Level 2 – Infrastructure	Compliance Auditing	Individual Professional Development Skilled People Identified and Recruited	Professional Practices and Processes Framework Audit Plan Based on Management/ Stakeholder Priorities	IA Operating Budget IA Business Plan	Managing within the IA Activity	Full Access to the Organization's Information, Assets, and People Reporting Relationships Established
Level 1 – Initial	Ad hoc and unstructured; isolated single audits or reviews of documents and transactions for accuracy and compliance; outputs dependent upon the skills of specific individuals holding the position; no specific professional practices established other than those provided by professional associations; funding approved by management, as needed; absence of infrastructure; auditors likely part of a larger organizational unit; no established capabilities; therefore, no specific key process areas					

2.2 The Elements of Internal Auditing

The following six essential elements were identified for an IA activity:

1. Services and Role of Internal Auditing
2. People Management
3. Professional Practices
4. Performance Management and Accountability
5. Organizational Relationships and Culture
6. Governance Structures

The first four elements—Services and Role of Internal Auditing, People Management, Professional Practices, and Performance Management and Accountability—relate primarily to the management and practices of the IA activity itself. The last two elements—Organizational Relationships and Culture and Governance Structures— also include the IA activity's relationship with the organization that it supports and the internal and external environments.

Processes, referred to as KPAs in the IA-CM, relate to the six elements, can be found within each capability level, and are descriptors of what it means to achieve a particular level. The dark gray in **exhibit II.2** identifies the elements where the IA activity may have more opportunity to independently create and institutionalize the KPAs up to and including those found in Level 3 – Integrated. Detailed descriptions of the elements follow.

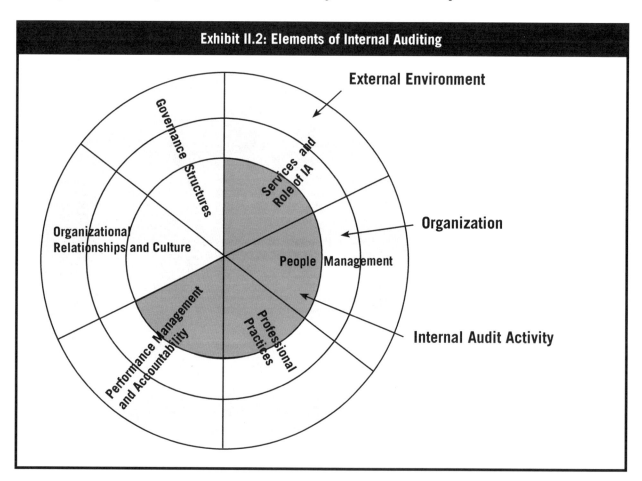

Exhibit II.2: Elements of Internal Auditing

2.2.1 Services and Role of Internal Auditing

The expected **role** of the IA activity to provide independent and objective assessments to assist the organization in accomplishing its objectives and improve operations—is found to some degree in most IA activities in the public sector. However, the means by which this role is accomplished or the services provided varies among different jurisdictions and environments. The services provided are typically based on the organization's needs and the IA activity's authority, scope, and capacity.

Services include the provision of assurance and consulting/advisory activities and can consist of audits of transactions, compliance, systems, processes, operations, performance/value-for-money, information and related technology, and financial statements and systems.

Services can also include the capability to assess and advise on organizational governance, risk management strategies/practices, and control processes.

The broadest audit focus "considers the organization's governance activities, which can help the organization achieve its objectives and priority goals and improve its governance framework, including its ethical code. The narrowest audit focus involves testing individual transactions for errors or for compliance with contract terms, policies, regulations, or laws. The auditors' scope of work can vary between these extremes and include activities such as reviewing internal controls, processes, and systems to identify systemic weaknesses and propose operational improvements."[10]

The services can be performed by the IA activity itself, co-sourced with external service providers, or outsourced.

2.2.2 People Management

People management is the process of creating a work environment that enables people to perform to the best of their abilities. People management is the system that begins when a job is defined as needed.

People management includes:

- Identifying specific attributes and developing clear job descriptions for each level of internal auditor.
- Recruiting appropriate people through an appropriate selection process.
- Identifying job requirements and work objectives based on performance standards, outcomes, and measures.
- Providing effective orientation, continuing education, professional development, and training.
- Providing ongoing coaching and continuous feedback, and conducting regular performance development discussions.
- Designing effective compensation and recognition systems that reward people for their contributions.
- Providing appropriate promotional and career development opportunities.

---

[10] *The Role of Auditing in Public Sector Governance*, 2nd Edition (Lake Mary, FL: The Institute of Internal Auditors, January 2012), 20.

2.2.3 Professional Practices

Professional practices reflects the full backdrop of policies, processes, and practices that enables the IA activity to be performed effectively and with proficiency and due professional care.

It includes the development and use of innovative and evolving frameworks/policies and their application to internal audit programs and operations.

It also refers to the capacity of the IA activity to align itself with the organization's priorities and risk management strategies and contribute to continuous improvement of the IA activity and the organization.

It includes the development and maintenance of "a quality assurance and improvement program that covers all aspects of the internal audit activity."[11]

2.2.4 Performance Management and Accountability

Performance management and accountability refers to the information needed to manage, conduct, and control the operations of the IA activity and account for its performance and results. It refers to the identification and communication of sufficient and relevant information to enable people to perform their assigned responsibilities.

This element includes the development and management of relevant information systems and financial and non-financial (operational and program) performance information. It includes the procedures to manage and protect the integrity of data and to produce and present the appropriate information and results when needed. It refers to reporting to relevant stakeholders and the public, where appropriate, on the effectiveness of the IA activity and its value contribution to the organization. It refers principally to management information, which can also be found integrated in and flowing from the other elements of internal auditing.

2.2.5 Organizational Relationships and Culture

Organizational relationships and culture refers to the organizational structure and internal management and relationships within the IA activity itself. It also refers to the IA activity's positioning within the organization's administrative infrastructure and management regime and its relationships with other units in the organization. It includes the IA activity's position in the Three Lines of Defense model and its relationship with the first and second lines of defense. Within the administrative infrastructure, it includes how the organization's policies, processes, and practices are interpreted and may impact on the IA activity's ability to effectively accomplish its objectives, including its capacity to access the information and people needed in the conduct of its work. It includes the CAE's relationships with senior management, and as part of the management team, as well as the ability to advise and influence top-level management and develop effective and ongoing relationships.

This element refers to the organization's internal relationships and internal culture and environment, and how these relationships and organizational culture may impact on key stakeholders and others outside the organization, including the public. It also refers to the IA activity's relationships with other review groups, including the external or legislative auditor.

---

[11] Standard 1300: Quality Assurance and Improvement Program (Lake Mary, FL: The Institute of Internal Auditors, 2017).

2.2.6 Governance Structures

Governance generally refers to the combination of processes and structures implemented by the board [an organization's governing body] to inform, direct, manage, and monitor the activities of the organization toward the achievement of its objectives.[12]

Governance structures includes the administrative and functional reporting relationships of the IA activity. It includes the CAE's reporting relationship to the governing body and how the IA activity fits within the organization's structure and governance regime. It includes the means by which the independence and objectivity of the IA activity is assured; for example, through its formal mandate, legislated authority, and/or oversight mechanism such as an audit committee. It also refers to the policies and processes established to provide the necessary authority, support, and resources for the IA activity to carry out its duties and contribute to its effectiveness and independence.

2.3 The Capability Levels—Descriptions and Relationships among KPAs

This section describes each capability level in the IA-CM (see **exhibit II.3**) and identifies the capabilities and relationships among the KPAs at the specific level. For each capability level, an exhibit is included that highlights the purposes for each KPA within each element at the end of the description of each level.

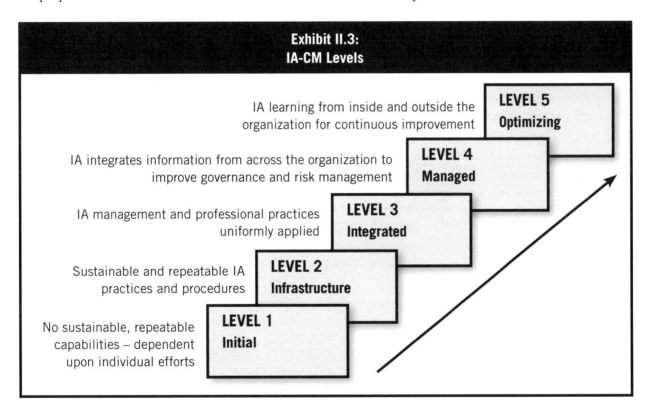

Exhibit II.3: IA-CM Levels

IA learning from inside and outside the organization for continuous improvement — **LEVEL 5 Optimizing**

IA integrates information from across the organization to improve governance and risk management — **LEVEL 4 Managed**

IA management and professional practices uniformly applied — **LEVEL 3 Integrated**

Sustainable and repeatable IA practices and procedures — **LEVEL 2 Infrastructure**

No sustainable, repeatable capabilities – dependent upon individual efforts — **LEVEL 1 Initial**

---

[12] *International Standards for the Professional Practice of Internal Auditing,* Glossary (Lake Mary, FL: The Institute of Internal Auditors, 2017).

2.3.1 Level 1 - Initial

Description of Level 1 and Risks Associated with Staying at That Level

At Level 1 – Initial, internal auditing is ad hoc or unstructured, few processes are defined, and practices are performed inconsistently. Isolated single audits and/or reviews of documents and transactions could be performed. Auditing is likely limited to transaction auditing; that is to say, examining the regularity and accuracy of individual economic transactions, or some basic compliance auditing.

The infrastructure for the IA activity has not been established and the auditors are likely part of a larger organizational unit. Funding is approved by management, as needed.

At this level, internal audit must rely on the individual efforts or personal skills of the auditors conducting the audits and their personal objectivity. There are no professional practices established other than those provided by professional associations.

In the absence of established key processes and practices, outputs are dependent upon the skills of the specific person holding the position. There is no certainty that such accomplishments would be repeatable or sustainable.

At Level 1, the organization faces the risk of not being able to rely on or routinely benefit from the value-added contribution of internal audit. Because of the lack of infrastructure and institutional capacity, the Initial Level, unlike other levels in the IA-CM, is not a level where it is desirable to remain, if internal audit is to be sustained and contribute in a reliable and consistent way to improving the organization's operations. The key question or challenge internal audit faces in progressing to Level 2 is how to establish and maintain repeatability of processes and thus a repeatable capability.

Moving from Level 1 to Level 2

Upward movement through the levels is dependent upon three variables—the capacity of the IA activity, the organization, and the overall public sector environment within which the organization operates. Specifically, to move from Level 1 to Level 2, certain prerequisites must exist in the environment and the organization to support the establishment of an IA activity.

For example, enabling factors in the environment would include:

- Government commitment to the importance of internal auditing.

- Legislation or government policy assuring the organizational independence of the IA activity and the personal objectivity of the internal auditors.

- Government culture supporting transparency, openness, and accountability for results.

- Strong financial management and control systems—such that there is an appropriate internal control framework within which internal audit can contribute.

- Mature corporate governance and risk management processes—where the benefits of oversight are recognized.

- History and tradition of external auditing—such that the concept of auditing is understood and the relationship between external and internal auditing can be appreciated.

Within the organization, the following would need to be demonstrated:

- Support for effective corporate governance processes, including oversight.

- Organizational and personal accountability for results—for example, where managers are held accountable for effective financial management and control as well as for operational results.

- Culture of professionalism to help appreciate the professionalism of internal audit.

- Public commitment by top-level management to internal audit, particularly as an independent provider of assurance and advisory services.

- Central driver—leader or champion for internal audit—to promote its role, an appropriate reporting relationship, and its independence.

- Demand by managers for internal audit services.

- Budget support to establish internal audit as a separate activity with appropriate human resource capabilities, including a CAE.

- Conducive environment facilitating access to the information, assets, and people needed to carry out the internal audit work.

Exhibit II.4 identifies seven attributes/key features in a government environment that may impact on the capacity to implement internal auditing in a lasting and effective way and the capability of an IA activity. It can be used to assess the likelihood that internal audit can move from Level 1 to Level 2 – Infrastructure.

Exhibit II.4: **Assessment of Government Environment**
1. Is the government stable?
Consider:
• The length of time the current government has been in place.
• The lowest level to which political appointments in the public service extend and how those positions could impact on policy making with respect to consistency and continuity.
• Orderly transition of governments among various political parties.
2. Is the legislative and regulatory environment structured but not overly burdensome?
Consider:
• The government's receptivity to introducing new legislation.
• Whether an operational separation exists between legislation/regulations and standards/policies/ guidelines to allow efficiency and flexibility.

Exhibit II.4: (continued)   **Assessment of Government Environment**

3. Have corporate governance and risk management structures and processes been established that include external oversight?

Consider:

- The extent of external oversight by elected bodies.
- The role and effectiveness of the Supreme Audit Institution and other national external oversight bodies.
- Whether the government appears to be embracing risk management strategies.

4. Have comprehensive financial management and control systems been established, including internal audit?

Consider:

- The government's appetite for reform and the degree that administrative and financial management reform has been achieved.
- Whether there is a central government ministry to lead and provide guidance for financial management reform.
- Whether there are central policies/ standards for accounting, financial reporting etc.
- Whether there are central drivers for internal audit.

5. Does the government culture support public transparency, accountability, and ethical behavior?

Consider:

- Whether there are corporate codes of conduct and recourse mechanisms.
- The extent to which the public service recruitment process is transparent and has established standards and procedures.
- The extent to which the public is informed of government processes and results.

6. Has the government embraced managerial accountability for results?

Consider:

- Whether there are clear lines of accountability within levels of government and among ministries.
- Whether there are clearly identified responsibilities and lines of accountability for individual managers within ministries and organizational units.

7. Is the reputation/status of the government sector and its public servants viewed positively?

Consider:

- Whether public sector managers are respected for their positions and work.
- Whether salaries for government administrative/professional positions are comparable to those of the quasi-public and private sectors.
- The number of vacant positions and the interest in applying for the positions.
- The ability to attract and retain qualified persons (e.g., salary scales, working conditions, benefits, etc.).

To achieve capability Level 2, it is critical that the appropriate administrative and management infrastructures are established for the IA activity to support and maintain the repeatability of processes and sustainability of capabilities.

For internal audit to move from Level 1– Initial to Level 2 – Infrastructure, the "essential activities" identified in each KPA at Level 2 must be carried out to accomplish the specific purpose of that KPA. In this respect, certain practices must be mastered and institutionalized into the IA activity to achieve each of the KPAs at Level 2. All the KPAs at Level 2 must be institutionalized for the IA activity to be considered at capability Level 2.

2.3.2 Level 2 – Infrastructure

Overview of the Capabilities and Relationships Among KPAs

At Level 2 – Infrastructure, the primary objective is to instill a process discipline into the IA activity that ensures that basic internal audit practices and processes are performed on a regular and repeatable basis. To do so, the IA activity is initiating the development of its management and administrative infrastructures. An audit charter establishing the purpose, authority, and responsibility of the IA activity and its reporting relationship (administrative and functional) within the organization is developed. Organizational policies are being established that provide for the IA activity's full access to the organization's information, assets, and people to conduct its work.

In addition, legislation (national, state, or local) requiring internal auditing may be enacted providing the foundation upon which to build the IA activity. However, at this level, such legislation and policies may not necessarily provide for the full authority and broad scope of the IA activity.

At the Infrastructure Level, the IA activity primarily conducts control-based or traditional compliance auditing; in other words, audits of conformity and adherence of a particular area, process, or system to policies, plans, procedures, laws, regulations, contracts, or other requirements. These could include financial audits as well as system or process audits that assess whether an appropriate internal control framework is in place and operating.

The IA activity has started to identify and recruit people with the necessary competencies and relevant skills to carry out the work. However, to some extent, there continues to be reliance on individual people and their personal skills and competencies. Emphasis is placed on individuals taking responsibility for their own professional development to ensure that they continuously maintain and enhance their professional capabilities.

Public and professional sources of knowledge are identified and available to support the IA activity meet its professional obligations. A professional practices and processes framework is being developed which includes documented policies, processes, and procedures to encourage consistent application of internal audit guidance and practices across the IA activity. However, all the relevant internal audit policies, processes, and practices may not have been institutionalized, and the IA activity may fall short of meeting some major objectives. For example, the IA activity may not have sufficient organizational independence, and may not have fully implemented a quality assurance and improvement program (which includes ongoing internal monitoring as well as periodic internal and external quality assessments).

The management effort of the IA activity is primarily focused on its own operations and relationships, such as organizational structure, budget preparation and monitoring, annual planning, providing the necessary audit tools and technology, and performing audits. Interactions with organizational managers are focused on carrying out the business of the IA activity.

In this respect, the IA activity develops its periodic (annual or multiyear) plans for which audits and/or other services will be provided, based on management's priorities through consultations with management and/or other stakeholders.

The IA activity has been allocated its own operating budget. It prepares a periodic business plan for delivering the services of the IA activity, including administrative and support services.

At Level 2, there will be some significant opportunities for improving the effectiveness of the IA activity, and as such, it will only partially conform with the *Standards*. However, there may be environmental and organizational factors impacting on the ability of the IA activity to progress to a higher capability level, and this may be the most appropriate level for that IA activity in that organization within that particular environment.

Exhibit II.5 highlights the purposes for each KPA within each element at Level 2.

Exhibit II.5: Purposes of the KPAs at Level 2—Infrastructure		
Element	**KPA**	**Purpose**
Services and Role of IA	**Compliance Auditing**	To carry out an audit of conformity and adherence of a particular area, process, or system to policies, plans, procedures, laws, regulations, contracts, or other requirements that govern the conduct of the area, process, or system subject to audit.
People Management	**Skilled People Identified and Recruited**	To identify and attract people with the necessary competencies and relevant skills to carry out the work of the IA activity. Appropriately qualified and recruited internal auditors are more likely to provide credibility to the internal audit results.
	Individual Professional Development	To ensure that internal auditors continuously maintain and enhance their professional capabilities.
Professional Practices	**Audit Plan Based on Management/ Stakeholders' Priorities**	To develop periodic (annual or multiyear) plans for which audits and/or other services will be provided, based on consultations with management and/or other stakeholders.

		Exhibit II.5: (continued)
		Purposes of the KPAs at Level 2—Infrastructure

Element	KPA	Purpose
Professional Practices (continued)	**Professional Practices and Processes Framework**	To help facilitate the performance of audit engagements with the independence and objectivity and proficiency and due professional care envisaged in the internal audit charter and the Mission of Internal Audit, the Definition of Internal Auditing, the Code of Ethics, the Core Principles, and the *Standards*. The professional practices and processes framework includes the policies, processes, and procedures that will guide the IA activity in managing its operations; developing its internal audit work program; and planning, performing, and reporting on the results of internal audits.
Performance Management and Accountability	**Internal Audit Business Plan**	To establish a periodic plan for delivering the services of the IA activity, including administrative and support services, and the expected results.
	Internal Audit Operating Budget	To be allocated and use its own operating budget to plan the services of the IA activity.
Organizational Relationships and Culture	**Managing Within the IA Activity**	To focus the management effort of the IA activity on its own operations and relationships within the activity itself, such as organizational structure, people management, budget preparation and monitoring, annual planning, providing the necessary audit tools and technology, and performing audits. Interactions with organizational managers are focused on carrying out the business of the IA activity.
Governance Structures	**Reporting Relationships Established**	To establish formal reporting relationships (administrative and functional) for the IA activity.
	Full Access to the Organization's Information, Assets, and People	To provide the authority for the IA activity to obtain access to all the information, assets, and people that it requires to carry out its duties.

2.3.3 Level 3 – Integrated

Overview of the Capabilities and Relationships among KPAs

The objective of Level 3 – Integrated is to capitalize on processes that work best, standardize and integrate them into day-to-day operations, and eliminate wide variations in performance.

At Level 3, all relevant internal audit policies, processes, and procedures are defined, documented, and integrated into each other and the organization's infrastructure. Internal audit management and professional practices are well established and uniformly applied across the IA activity. The IA activity has a clear understanding of the efficient and effective alignment of auditor capabilities, current practices, and current enabling technologies.

At this level, the IA activity focuses on its capacity, its organizational independence, and the personal objectivity of its auditors. The administrative and functional reporting relationship of the IA activity continues to evolve. To further strengthen the CAE's independence, a direct functional reporting relationship to the governing body has been established along with a direct administrative reporting relationship to either the chief executive officer (CEO) or governing body.[13]

A mechanism/process has also been established by management to provide oversight and advice to the IA activity, review its results, and ensure appropriate actions are taken to strengthen its independence. Operating managers respect audit independence, are responsive to audit requests, and provide constructive feedback to facilitate the audit process. Involvement of a variety of managers in the decisions related to the IA activity helps to extend the activity's support and scope beyond a single individual and helps ensure its independence.

A formal funding mechanism has been established that will enable the IA activity to be appropriately financed. It can set its own priorities to address the identified engagements included in its risk-based audit and services plan.

A key aspect of Level 3 is the changing role of internal audit. The role evolves from performing only traditional internal audit services to integrating as a team player and providing advice on performance and management of risks. Internal audit is evolving to a "value-added" activity that helps an organization manage its risks and take advantage of opportunities to improve. The IA activity also pays attention to other topics, including organizational strategy and soft controls. Internal audit services have become more varied to support the needs of the organization's management.

The IA activity conducts process-based auditing, including performance or value-for-money audits that cover the full spectrum of operating and business processes, the associated management controls, and the results achieved. Advisory services are also undertaken by the IA activity to provide guidance and advice to management in a focused and timely fashion. The IA activity will leverage information technology to improve audit operations; for example, through working paper storage, auditor collaboration, audit report writing, and data analytics.

However, at this level, the IA activity will not be providing overall assurance on the organization's governance, risk management, and control processes as a whole. It will be performing individual engagements on operations, activities, programs, and processes throughout the organization.

---

[13] According to the Glossary in the *Standards* (January 2017), the definition of Board is "The highest level of governing body (e.g., a board of directors, a supervisory board, or a board of governors or trustees) charged with the responsibility to direct and/or oversee the organization's activities and hold senior management accountable. Although governance arrangements vary among jurisdictions and sectors, typically the board includes members who are not part of management. If a board does not exist, the word "board" in the *Standards* refers to a group or person charged with governance of the organization. Furthermore, "board" in the *Standards* may refer to a committee or another body to which the governing body has delegated certain functions (e.g., an audit committee)."

The IA activity ensures that the right people are recruited, retained, motivated, and developed to help meet its business objectives. It is staffed with professionally qualified people, including those from various disciplines. An internal audit competency framework (career progression of positions and responsibilities from entry level to manager) has been created to support professional growth and development. There is a training and development plan for each individual to guide improvement and progress through the competency framework. Auditors are encouraged to be involved in professional associations. Team building and team competency development is becoming more important for performing more complex internal audit assignments. As such, criteria for effective teamwork behaviors and practices, along with communication and critical/strategic thinking skills, are incorporated into the staff competency framework.

At this level, the IA activity is starting to align itself with the organization's business and the risks it faces. It systematically assesses risks and focuses its periodic audit and services plan on risk exposures throughout the organization. Development of the plan is coordinated with the human resource levels authorized to the IA activity to ensure that identified risks and priorities are appropriately addressed. The IA activity considers other resourcing strategies (e.g., recruitment, co-sourcing, outsourcing, etc.), as necessary, when the internal audit capacity is not sufficient in the IA activity.

The IA activity is seen as an integral component of the organization. The CAE is regarded as a valued member of the management team and participates in appropriate management activities of the organization. For example, the CAE is included in communications and forums of the management team, and as an observer, is able to maintain a channel of communication with senior management.

On behalf of senior management, the IA activity liaises with and coordinates the work of the external or legislative auditor. To further support management, the IA activity shares relevant information and coordinates activities with other internal and external providers of assurance and advisory services to ensure appropriate organizational coverage and minimize duplication of effort. The IA activity also supports the implementation and coordination of an effective Three Lines of Defense model within the organization to facilitate an understanding of its importance and the respective roles and responsibilities of the various risk and control functions.

Other KPAs at this level focus on the IA activity's capacity to monitor and assess the effectiveness of its operations. The IA activity will have planning and reporting mechanisms to ensure that resources are allocated appropriately to meet objectives and operations are performed efficiently and economically. The necessary information, including both financial and non-financial information, will be received and used to manage the IA activity's day-to-day operations, support decision-making, and demonstrate accountability.

The IA activity develops meaningful indicators and measures that enable it to assess its performance and routinely monitor progress against targets to ensure that results are achieved as intended. In addition, it will have developed a process to monitor and assess the overall effectiveness of its quality assurance and improvement program. This process will include ongoing internal monitoring of the performance of the IA activity as well as periodic internal and external quality assessments.

At Level 3, the IA activity will generally conform with the *Standards*.

Exhibit II.6 highlights the purposes for each KPA within each element at Level 3.

	Exhibit II.6: Purposes of the KPAs at Level 3—Integrated	
Element	**KPA**	**Purpose**
Services and Role of IA	**Performance/ Value-for-Money Audits**	To assess and report on the efficiency, effectiveness, and economy of operations, activities, or programs; or conduct engagements on governance, risk management, and control. Performance/value-for-money auditing covers the full spectrum of operating and business processes, the associated management controls, and the results achieved.
	Advisory Services	To analyze a situation and/or provide guidance and advice to management. Advisory services add value without the internal auditor assuming management responsibility. Advisory services are those that are directed toward facilitation rather than assurance and include training, systems development reviews, performance and control self-assessment, counseling, and advice.
People Management	**Workforce Coordination**	To coordinate the development of the periodic audit and services plan to the human resource levels authorized to the IA activity. Because resources are often constrained, the IA activity needs to use appropriate methods to set priorities on planned projects and services to limit its commitments to a "doable" quantity and type of projects and services.
	Professionally Qualified Staff	To staff the IA activity with professionally qualified staff and retain the individuals who have demonstrated a minimum level of competence.
	Team Building and Capacity	To develop staff members' capacity to function effectively in a team environment, beginning with focus on the individual project team. Because many public sector audits cover scopes that require the concerted effort of a team of auditors to conduct, and because the skills needed to conduct an audit are not necessarily the same skills needed to work effectively in a group environment, additional team competencies are required.

Exhibit II.6: (continued)		
Purposes of the KPAs at Level 3—Integrated		
Element	**KPA**	**Purpose**
Professional Practices	**Risk-Based Audit Plans**	To systematically assess risks and focus the priorities of the IA activity's periodic audit and services plan on risk exposures throughout the organization.
	Quality Management Framework	To establish and maintain processes to continuously monitor, assess, and improve the effectiveness of the IA activity. Processes include ongoing internal monitoring of the performance of the IA activity as well as periodic internal and external quality assessments.
Performance Management and Accountability	**IA Management Reports**	To receive and use information to manage the IA activity's day-to-day operations, support decision-making, and demonstrate accountability.
	Cost Information	To provide sufficient information from the financial tracking system so that the IA activity understands the cost information sufficiently to use it to manage its services as economically and efficiently as possible. This practice goes slightly beyond budget variances and integrates the relationship of outputs to inputs.
	Performance Measures	In addition to cost data, to develop meaningful indicators and measures that enable the IA activity to measure and report on its performance and routinely monitor its progress against targets to ensure that results are achieved as economically and efficiently as possible. These will be primarily process and input measures, and some output or qualitative outcome measures.
Organizational Relationships and Culture	**Integral Component of Management Team**	To participate in the organization's management activities in some form as a valued member of the management team. Although the CAE does not carry out management's responsibilities, the CAE is included in communications and forums of the management team, and as an observer, is able to maintain a channel of communication with senior management.
	Coordination with Other Review Groups	To share information and coordinate activities with other internal and external providers of assurance and advisory services to ensure appropriate organizational coverage and minimize duplication of effort.

Element	KPA	Purpose
Exhibit II.6: (continued) **Purposes of the KPAs at Level 3—Integrated**		
Governance Structures	**Funding Mechanisms**	To establish a robust and transparent funding process that ensures adequate resources to allow the IA activity to discharge its obligations.
	Management Oversight and Support of the IA Activity	To establish a mechanism/process within the organization to provide oversight and advice to the IA activity, review its results, and ensure appropriate actions are taken to strengthen its independence. Operating managers respect audit independence, are responsive to audit requests, and provide constructive feedback to facilitate the audit process. Involvement of a variety of managers in the decisions related to the IA activity helps to extend the activity's support and scope beyond a single individual and helps ensure its independence.
	CAE Reports to Top-Level Authority	To strengthen the CAE's independence by establishing a direct functional reporting relationship to the governing body and a direct administrative reporting relationship to either the chief executive officer (CEO) or governing body.

2.3.4 Level 4 – Managed

Overview of the Capabilities and Relationships among KPAs

At Level 4 – Managed, the governance structure of the IA activity has evolved significantly. There is an independent oversight body, including members independent of the organization's management, to assure the independence of the IA activity, broaden the activity's scope of input and influence, and help to strengthen the organization's accountability.

Furthermore, the IA activity functions as an integral part of the organization's governance and risk management. The CAE is positioned to both formally and informally advise on strategic issues and influence top-level management. This professional relationship with top-level management, which fosters frank exchanges while maintaining independence and objectivity, facilitates the organization's understanding and appreciation of the vision, leadership, and foresight of the CAE and the contribution of the IA activity.

One objective at Level 4 is to set quantitative performance and quality targets and reduce the variation in processes that contribute to achieving the targets. Performance metrics are in place to measure and monitor the internal audit processes and results. The IA activity has balanced and integrated its use of quantitative and qualitative data and information to help it achieve its strategic objectives and continuously improve its performance to address the need for greater value, efficiency, and effectiveness. The IA activity functions as a well-managed business unit.

In developing its periodic audit and services plan, the IA activity aligns, as appropriate, its engagements with the organization's management of risks. It quantitatively measures risks to the organization and takes into consideration the organization's enterprise risk management strategies and practices.[14]

The IA activity has developed a framework broad enough to encompass risk and control considerations at all levels of the organization's governance, risk management, and control processes.

The IA activity integrates the information obtained from its work throughout the organization to make informed observations and recommendations on cost versus quality and risk versus opportunities. In this way, the IA activity helps the organization balance among its competing objectives and establish cost-effective control and risk management practices.

At Level 4, the IA activity and its key stakeholders' expectations are in alignment. As a result, the IA activity is recognized as delivering significant contributions to the organization through its value-added services; for example, as a catalyst for strengthening the organization's control performance.

At this level, the IA activity has the requisite skills and competencies in place, including knowledge and skill specialization areas of expertise, as required (e.g., information technology, fraud, governance, risk management, etc.) with a capacity for renewal and knowledge sharing within the activity and across the organization. It has sufficiently planned and coordinated its workforce activities to ensure it has the professional capacity to meet the organization's current business needs.

The IA activity provides leadership and professional development opportunities for internal audit staff by supporting their involvement and participation in professional bodies. The organization and the IA activity pursue a strategy together that integrates the development of the organization's managers with the training and experiences of the IA activity and vice versa. For example, a training and development program could be put in place in the IA activity that provides high-potential employees with broad exposure to business activities, corporate culture, the control environment, and risk management practices, leading to managerial positions throughout the organization.

The internal audit services and role are also expanding significantly at this level. The IA activity's use of technology has matured, with multiple forms of technology enabling audit operations. Its knowledge management program now leverages specialized auditor skills and includes the development of formalized tools/resource library. In addition to providing opinions on the effectiveness of operations, the IA activity is now also assessing the efficiency of processes supported by, for example, data analytics and process mining. Strategic risk audits may also be performed as well as the effectiveness of soft controls.

The IA activity is now conducting sufficient work to provide an opinion on the overall adequacy and effectiveness of the organization's governance, risk management, and control processes. The IA activity has coordinated its audit services to be sufficiently comprehensive so that it can provide reasonable assurance at a corporate level that these processes are adequate and functioning as intended to meet the organization's objectives.

Exhibit II.7 highlights the purposes for each KPA within each element at Level 4.

---

[14] Risk management is "a process to identify, assess, manage, and control potential events or situations to provide reasonable assurance regarding the achievement of the organization's objectives." *International Standards for the Professional Practice of Internal Auditing*, Glossary (Lake Mary, FL: The Institute of Internal Auditors, 2017).

	Exhibit II.7: **Purposes of the KPAs at Level 4—Managed**	
Element	**KPA**	**Purpose**
Services and Role of IA	**Overall Assurance on Governance, Risk Management, and Control**	To conduct sufficient work to provide an opinion on the overall adequacy and effectiveness of the organization's governance, risk management, and control processes. The IA activity has coordinated its audit services to be sufficiently comprehensive that it can provide reasonable assurance at a corporate level that these processes are adequate and functioning as intended to meet the organization's objectives.
People Management	**Workforce Planning**	To coordinate workforce activities to achieve current business needs of the IA activity. Workforce planning involves developing a workforce plan that sets out the resources, skills, training, and tools required to conduct the audits that have been identified (or are proposed) in the periodic audit and services plan.
	IA Activity Supports Professional Bodies	To provide leadership and professional development opportunities for the internal audit staff by supporting their involvement and participation in professional bodies.
	IA Contributes to Management Development	To integrate the development of the organization's managers with the training and experiences of the IA activity and vice versa. The organization and the IA activity pursue a strategy to encourage people with a good understanding of governance, risk management, and controls to work and contribute throughout the organization.
Professional Practices	**Audit Strategy Leverages Organization's Management of Risks**	To link the IA activity's periodic audit and services plan with the organization's enterprise risk management strategies and practices.
Performance Management and Accountability	**Integration of Qualitative and Quantitative Performance Measures**	To enable the IA activity to use information on performance to measure and monitor fluctuations that affect its results. The activity has balanced its use of quantitative and qualitative data to help it achieve its strategic objectives.

	Exhibit II.7: (continued)	
	Purposes of the KPAs at Level 4—Managed	
Element	**KPA**	**Purpose**
Organizational Relationships and Culture	**CAE Advises and Influences Top-Level Management**	To facilitate the organization's understanding and appreciation of the vision, leadership, and foresight of the CAE, and to develop a professional relationship with top-level management that fosters frank exchanges, while maintaining independence and objectivity. Senior management values the CAE for advice on strategic issues.
Governance Structures	**Independent Oversight of the IA Activity**	To establish an oversight body, including members independent of the organization's management, to assure the independence of the IA activity, broaden the activity's scope of input and influence, and help to strengthen the organization's accountability.

2.3.5 Level 5 – Optimizing

Overview of the Capabilities and Relationships among KPAs

At Level 5 – Optimizing, the focus is on learning for continuous improvement to enhance capability. An IA activity at Level 5 is characterized as a learning organization with continuous process improvements and innovation. It monitors the changing external environment and uses information from inside and outside the organization to refine its approaches to assessing governance, risk management, and control. By providing advice on emerging trends and organization-wide issues, the IA activity contributes to organizational learning and improvement and encourages the development of innovative business practices and processes to help the organization achieve its strategic business objectives.

The IA activity's governance structure is fully developed. Its independence, power, and authority are fully actualized (for example, through legislation, formal mandate, statutory policy, and/or independent oversight body). The IA activity is not a discretionary policy of management. It has uncompromising independence, power, and authority to determine the scope of internal auditing, perform its work, and communicate its results. It has the stability and independence and enterprise-wide perspective to focus on future directions and continuous improvement for both the IA activity and the organization.

The IA activity is a critical part of the organization's governance structure. The IA activity leads in contributing to improvements in the organization's risk management and control environment, for example, through supporting management coordinate and strengthen its first and second lines of defense functions.

The CAE continues to maintain and develop effective relationships with management and key stakeholders, including the independent oversight body, to ensure that their needs and expectations are aligned with the services of the IA activity, and that the visibility and contribution of the IA activity is evident. The words and actions of senior management, the oversight body, and all key stakeholders demonstrate full acceptance for and support of the IA activity.

Individual, unit, and organizational performance measures are fully integrated to drive performance improvements in the IA activity. Further, the IA activity integrates the performance data, global best practices, and feedback received from its ongoing quality assurance and improvement program processes to continuously strengthen and develop its capacity to deliver world-class internal auditing. Technology is optimally aligned to enable audit operations and produce high-level reporting. The IA activity also explores and assesses leading internal audit practices in other jurisdictions to further enhance its organizational independence and the personal objectivity of its auditors.

In addition to having comprehensive performance metrics to monitor and improve its performance, the IA activity reports to the organization's stakeholders and the public, where appropriate, on its effectiveness and its value contribution to the organization. The IA activity identifies its impact made with the resources provided to it; measures the value to the organization produced from its efficient and effectively-aligned people, processes and technology; and demonstrates its transparency and accountability for results.

The IA activity has top-level professional and specialized skills, a fully developed knowledge management program that effectively leverages those skills, and has sufficiently developed its leadership capacity to provide foresight and serve as a catalyst to achieve positive change in the organization. It also supports and facilitates its leaders to become key leaders in relevant professional bodies—as thought leaders to influence the growth and evolution of the profession and apply forward-thinking innovative practices in the organization.

The IA activity understands the organization's strategic directions and emerging issues and risks. It evolves its business requirements, workforce development needs (including resources and skillsets), risk assessment strategies, and processes to meet the organization's potential future needs.

The role of the IA activity now encompasses a stronger performance orientation through continuous customer service, business partnerships, independent advice, and advisory services. It is recognized as influencing positive change and continuous improvement to business processes, bottom-line results, and accountability within the organization. The IA activity is seen as a trusted advisor.

Exhibit II.8 highlights the purposes for each KPA within each element at Level 5.

Exhibit II.8: Purposes of the KPAs at Level 5—Optimizing		
Element	**KPA**	**Purpose**
Services and Role of IA	**IA Recognized as Key Agent of Change**	To have sufficiently developed the professional and leadership capacity of the IA activity to provide foresight and serve as a catalyst to achieve positive change in the organization.
People Management	**Workforce Projection**	To coordinate long-term workforce development activities to meet future business needs of the IA activity. Workforce projection involves developing a strategic workforce plan that sets out the IA activity's objectives for competency development and workforce activities, in conjunction with the organization's projected strategic needs, and developing plans to guide workforce development activities for the IA activity.

	Exhibit II.8: (continued)	
	Purposes of the KPAs at Level 5—Optimizing	
Element	**KPA**	**Purpose**
People Management (continued)	**Leadership Involvement with Professional Bodies**	To facilitate and support top leaders of the IA activity becoming key leaders within relevant professional bodies. In addition to making contributions to the profession through their volunteer work, the CAE and other internal auditors will become thought leaders and influence the growth and evolution of the profession. Participating in the administration and/or leadership of professional bodies helps auditors learn and practice higher-level people skills, since their roles vis-à-vis their colleagues require different means of interacting from their "auditor" or "manager" role within their own organization.
Professional Practices	**Strategic IA Planning**	To understand the organization's strategic directions and emerging issues and risks, and change the IA activity's skillsets and audit services to meet potential future needs.
	Continuous Improvement in Professional Practices	To integrate the performance data, global leading practices, and feedback received from ongoing quality assurance and improvement program processes to continuously strengthen and develop the IA activity's capacity to deliver world-class internal auditing.
Performance Management and Accountability	**Outcome Performance and Value to Organization Achieved**	To report on the effectiveness of the IA activity to demonstrate transparency and accountability to the organization's stakeholders and the public and identify the contribution and impact made by the IA activity with the resources provided.
Organizational Relationships and Culture	**Effective and Ongoing Relationships**	To use strong relationship management skills of the CAE for maintaining appropriate visibility and alignment with key stakeholders, management, and audit committee needs and expectations.
Governance Structures	**Independence, Power, and Authority of the IA Activity**	To fully actualize the IA activity's independence, power, and authority.

3. Applying and Interpreting the IA-CM

The following section provides some principles, factors, and issues to consider when applying and interpreting the IA-CM.

3.1 Principles in Applying the IA-CM

- Professional judgment is needed to apply and interpret the IA-CM.
- A process or practice cannot be improved if it cannot be repeated. Therefore, it is not sustainable.
- A KPA is achieved when it is institutionalized into the culture of the IA activity.
- All KPAs, up to and including the KPAs at a given capability level, must be institutionalized to achieve that level.
- An IA activity may choose to stay at a particular level.
- The IA-CM is intended primarily as a self-assessment exercise for continuous improvement.

3.2 Environmental and Organizational Factors

The model recognizes how the external regulatory environment and the public sector organization itself may impact on the capability of the IA activity. For example, there may be factors in the environment that influence whether an IA activity can develop and evolve, including the existence of an effective legal and legislative framework, established financial management and control processes, and a strong human resource component.

Within the organization, it is important to understand the influence of corporate governance, organizational culture, internal control systems, human resource capacities, and the demand and need for the IA activity. In addition, other organizational factors such as size, nature, complexity, and risks of operations must be considered when assessing whether and how a particular KPA is implemented and institutionalized.

In using the IA-CM, it is important to determine "what makes sense" and is reasonable considering the organization and environment. For example, the element, organizational relationships and culture, may be influenced by the organization's scope and complexity. If the organization's operations are relatively limited and its program less complex to administer, its CEO may have a fairly narrow span of control. In such cases, there may be more opportunity for the CAE to directly influence top-level management. In addition, IA activities in smaller organizations may be able to implement a particular KPA without the bureaucratic infrastructure of larger organizations.

3.3 Capability Level Issues

3.3.1 Is Level 3 Sufficient for an IA Activity?

An IA activity at capability Level 3 – Integrated will generally conform with the *Standards* and focus its efforts on capacity, independence, and objectivity. While capability levels in the IA-CM provide a road map for continuous improvement, an IA activity may choose to remain at Level 3. However, it is important that the IA activity not become complacent at Level 3. The external environment, the organization's culture and business processes, or the makeup of the IA activity may change. It needs to ensure that the KPAs, up to and including those in

Level 3, remain institutionalized and continuously improve on the quality of those processes through refining the institutionalizing practices, if necessary.

3.3.2 Why and When to Aspire to Level 4 or Level 5?

The IA activity cannot outpace the maturity of the organization that it supports. For example, to implement KPAs at Level 4, such as "Overall Assurance on Governance, Risk Management, and Control," senior management will have had to establish a framework that supports an assertion or representation on the effectiveness of its governance, risk management, and control processes and expect an overall opinion in this respect from the IA activity. Further, to institutionalize the KPA "Audit Strategy Leverages Organization's Management of Risks," the organization will have had to establish enterprise risk-management strategies and practices. At Level 5, to institutionalize "IA Recognized as Key Agent of Change," the organization will have to visibly support and make a strong commitment to endorse internal audit's key role in influencing change in the organization. The KPAs in Level 4 and Level 5 require environmental and organizational influences to effectively institutionalize them into the IA activity.

3.3.3 Can Capability Levels Be Skipped?

Implementation of the KPAs at one level establishes the basis for the practices and capabilities at the next level and provides the foundation upon which to progress to the next level. Hence, it is a "building block" approach to establishing effective internal audit in an organization. Without building an appropriate foundation at one level for implementing a KPA at the next level, that KPA may not be sustainable or achieve the outputs and outcomes desired. With the exception of Level 1– Initial, it is not possible to skip levels.

3.3.4 Can KPAs Be Ignored?

All KPAs should be considered as relevant. While KPAs are expressed at a single capability level, there are relationships that stretch across the elements and through the capability levels. An IA activity might want to ignore a KPA as not relevant to its organization or environment. However, it is important to give careful consideration before this is done. It may simply be that the particular KPA is difficult to implement. It is important to remember that the various KPAs form relationships through mutually supporting practices.

3.3.5 Must All Elements Be at the Same Capability Level?

It is not unusual for an IA activity to have strengths in one or more of the internal audit elements. For example, the organization and the IA activity may be focused on excellence in people management, and therefore, the IA activity has institutionalized all the KPAs up to and including Level 4 in people management. However, for an IA activity to achieve a given capability level, the KPAs in all elements up to and including that level must be institutionalized into the culture of the IA activity.

3.4 The IA-CM and a Quality Assurance and Improvement Program

Exhibit II.9 provides excerpts from the *Standards* (January 2017) relating to a quality assurance and improvement program. The program's primary purpose is to evaluate whether the IA activity conforms with the *Standards* and whether internal auditors apply the Code of Ethics. However, it does look at overall efficiency and effectiveness of the IA activity, whether and how it adds value, and identifies areas for improvement and leading practices.

The primary purpose of the IA-CM is as a self-assessment and development tool for public sector IA activities to determine the level of internal audit capability appropriate and optimum to their organization and environment. It describes an evolutionary path for a public sector organization to follow in developing effective internal auditing to meet its governance needs, taking into consideration the nature, complexity, and associated risks of the organization's operations.

> The IA-CM describes an evolutionary path for a public sector organization to follow in developing effective internal auditing to meet its governance needs, taking into consideration the nature, complexity, and associated risks of the organization's operations.

The IA-CM was intended for use globally with IA activities at all capability levels from start-up to world-class and from within various types of organizations in different public sector environments or governments.

The IA-CM is underpinned by the Mission of Internal Audit and the mandatory guidance (Definition of Internal Auditing, Code of Ethics, Core Principles, and the *Standards*) included in The IIA's International Professional Practices Framework (IPPF). However, it is not specifically evaluating conformance therewith, but rather whether key processes are repeatable, sustainable, and institutionalized into the IA activity.

During the global validation of the IA-CM, several of the IA activities had recently undergone an external quality assessment. More recently, IA-CM assessments have been performed for the purposes of conducting the self-assessment envisaged by Standard 1311: Internal Assessments.

When comparing the methodology and results of the external assessments to those of the IA-CM assessments, the overall results from both exercises appear to be in line with one another, where the IA-CM complemented the external quality assessment by having a broader scope in addition to assessing the underlying capabilities needed to meet the expectations of conformance with the *Standards*. Where a particular standard is not met, the IA-CM provides a road map for improvement.

Exhibit II.9:
Excerpts from Standards 1300 – 1312

1300 – Quality Assurance and Improvement Program

The chief audit executive must develop and maintain a quality assurance and improvement program that covers all aspects of the internal audit activity.

Interpretation:

A quality assurance and improvement program is designed to enable an evaluation of the internal audit activity's conformance with the Standards *and an evaluation of whether internal auditors apply the Code of Ethics. The program also assesses the efficiency and effectiveness of the internal audit activity and identifies opportunities for improvement. The chief audit executive should encourage board oversight in the quality assurance and improvement program.*

Exhibit II.9: (continued)
Excerpts from Standards 1300 – 1312

1310 – Requirements of the Quality Assurance and Improvement Program

The quality assurance and improvement program must include both internal and external assessments.

1311 – Internal Assessments

Internal Assessments must include:

- Ongoing monitoring of the performance of the internal audit activity.
- Periodic self-assessments or assessments by other persons within the organization with sufficient knowledge of internal audit practices.

Interpretation:

Ongoing monitoring is an integral part of the day-to-day supervision, review, and measurement of the internal audit activity. Ongoing monitoring is incorporated into the routine policies and practices used to manage the internal audit activity and uses processes, tools, and information considered necessary to evaluate conformance with the Code of Ethics and the Standards.

Periodic assessments are conducted to evaluate conformance with the Code of Ethics and the Standards.

Sufficient knowledge of internal audit practices requires at least an understanding of all elements of the International Professional Practices Framework.

1312 – External Assessments

External assessments must be conducted at least once every five years by a qualified, independent assessor or assessment team from outside the organization. The chief audit executive must discuss with the board:

- The form and frequency of external assessment.
- The qualifications and independence of the external assessor or assessment team, including any potential conflict of interest.

Interpretation:

External assessments may be accomplished through a full external assessment, or a self-assessment with independent external validation. The external assessor must conclude as to conformance with the Code of Ethics and the Standards*; the external assessment may also include operational or strategic comments.*

A qualified assessor or assessment team demonstrates competence in two areas: the professional practice of internal auditing and the external assessment process. Competence can be demonstrated through a mixture of experience and theoretical learning. Experience gained in organizations of similar size, complexity, sector or industry, and technical issues is more valuable than less relevant experience. In the case of an assessment team, not all members of the team need to have all the competencies; it is the team as a whole that is qualified. The chief audit executive uses professional judgment when assessing whether an assessor or assessment team demonstrates sufficient competence to be qualified.

An independent assessor or assessment team means not having either an actual or a perceived conflict of interest and not being a part of, or under the control of, the organization to which the internal audit activity belongs. The chief audit executive should encourage board oversight in the external assessment to reduce perceived or potential conflicts of interest.

4. Detailed Key Process Areas

The detailed description of each KPA identifies its purpose, essential activities, outputs, and outcomes. See **exhibit II.10**. Examples of institutionalizing practices are also included.

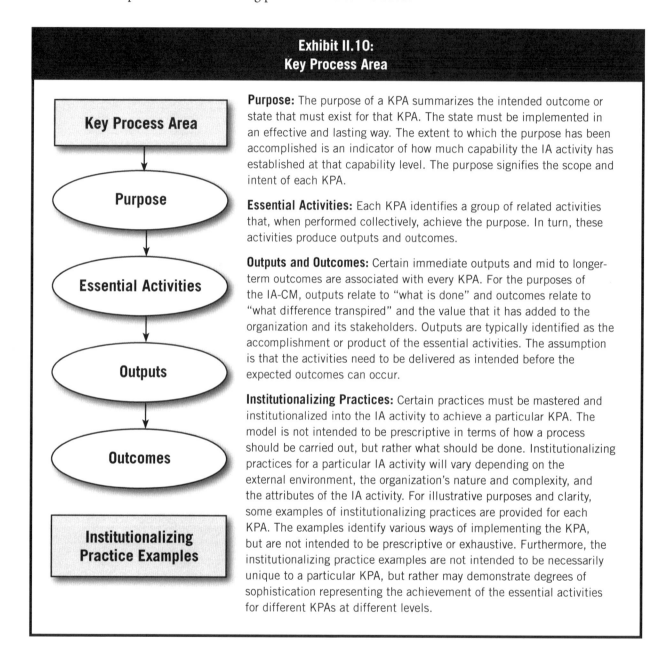

Exhibit II.10:
Key Process Area

Key Process Area

Purpose

Essential Activities

Outputs

Outcomes

Institutionalizing Practice Examples

Purpose: The purpose of a KPA summarizes the intended outcome or state that must exist for that KPA. The state must be implemented in an effective and lasting way. The extent to which the purpose has been accomplished is an indicator of how much capability the IA activity has established at that capability level. The purpose signifies the scope and intent of each KPA.

Essential Activities: Each KPA identifies a group of related activities that, when performed collectively, achieve the purpose. In turn, these activities produce outputs and outcomes.

Outputs and Outcomes: Certain immediate outputs and mid to longer-term outcomes are associated with every KPA. For the purposes of the IA-CM, outputs relate to "what is done" and outcomes relate to "what difference transpired" and the value that it has added to the organization and its stakeholders. Outputs are typically identified as the accomplishment or product of the essential activities. The assumption is that the activities need to be delivered as intended before the expected outcomes can occur.

Institutionalizing Practices: Certain practices must be mastered and institutionalized into the IA activity to achieve a particular KPA. The model is not intended to be prescriptive in terms of how a process should be carried out, but rather what should be done. Institutionalizing practices for a particular IA activity will vary depending on the external environment, the organization's nature and complexity, and the attributes of the IA activity. For illustrative purposes and clarity, some examples of institutionalizing practices are provided for each KPA. The examples identify various ways of implementing the KPA, but are not intended to be prescriptive or exhaustive. Furthermore, the institutionalizing practice examples are not intended to be necessarily unique to a particular KPA, but rather may demonstrate degrees of sophistication representing the achievement of the essential activities for different KPAs at different levels.

Services and Role of Internal Auditing

Level 2 – Infrastructure

Compliance Auditing

Purpose — To carry out an audit of conformity and adherence of a particular area, process, or system to policies, plans, procedures, laws, regulations, contracts, or other requirements that govern the conduct of the area, process, or system subject to audit.[15]

Essential Activities

- Include in the internal audit charter the nature of the assurance services provided to the organization.
- Plan the internal audit engagement:
  - Communicate with client management (e.g., through an audit engagement letter).
  - Identify the relevant authorities/criteria.
  - Obtain management acceptance of the audit criteria.
  - Document the control framework.
  - Review key controls and identify and assess engagement specific risks.
  - Identify the audit objectives, scope, and methodology (including sampling methodology).
  - Develop the detailed audit engagement plan.
- Perform the audit engagement:
  - Apply specific audit procedures.
  - Document the procedures performed and their results.
  - Evaluate the information obtained.
  - Draw specific conclusions and develop recommendations.
- Communicate the results of the audit engagement:
  - Prepare the report or other mechanism to communicate the engagement results.
  - Establish and maintain a system to monitor the disposition of results communicated to management (e.g., a follow-up process to ensure management actions have been effectively implemented or management has accepted the risk of not taking action).

Outputs

- Documented audit engagement results/report is provided to appropriate parties (including the external auditor, where relevant).
- Working-paper file that supports the audit conclusions and contents of the audit engagement product/report.
- Management action plan, if necessary.

Outcomes

- Assurance that the area, process, or system subject to audit operates in compliance with relevant authorities/criteria.
- Added value by identifying opportunities to improve the achievement of organizational objectives and the effectiveness of operations.
- Prevent, deter, and detect illegal acts or violations of established policies, procedures, or contract requirements.

Institutionalizing Practice Examples

- Internal audit charter includes the nature of the assurance services provided to the organization.
- Documented audit programs, procedures, and internal control questionnaires.
- Documented internal audit engagement guidelines.
- Internal audit engagement training.

---

[15] This includes the audit of financial transactions, including an evaluation of compliance with applicable statutes and regulations; the audit of the probity and propriety of administrative decisions taken within the audited entity; and any control-based internal auditing.

Services and Role of Internal Auditing

Level 3 – Integrated

Performance/Value-for-Money Audits

Purpose — To assess and report on the efficiency, effectiveness, and economy of operations, activities, or programs; or conduct engagements on governance, risk management, and control. Performance/value-for-money auditing covers the full spectrum of operating and business processes, the associated management controls, and the results achieved.

Essential Activities

- Include in the internal audit charter the nature of the assurance services provided to the organization and revise, as necessary.
- Plan the internal audit engagement:
  - o Communicate with client management.
  - o Understand the subject of the engagement, its environment, business objectives, etc.
  - o Identify and assess engagement-specific risks.
  - o Determine the objectives, scope, criteria, and approach of the audit engagement.[16]
  - o Develop the detailed audit engagement plan.
- Perform the audit engagement:
  - o Conduct specific audit tests or methodologies that are relevant to achieve the audit objectives.
  - o Draw specific conclusions and develop recommendations.
  - o Provide overall assurance and/or conclusions on the results of the audit engagement.
- Communicate the results of the audit engagement:
  - o Prepare the report or other mechanism to communicate the engagement results.
  - o Establish and maintain a system to monitor the disposition of results communicated to management (e.g., a follow-up process to ensure management actions have been effectively implemented or management has accepted the risk of not taking action).

Outputs

- Documented audit engagement results/report is provided to the appropriate parties (including the external auditor, where relevant).
- Working-paper file that supports the audit conclusions and contents of the audit engagement product/report.
- Management action plan, if necessary.

Outcomes

- Improved governance, risk management, and control processes of the subject of the audit engagement.
- Influencing change to contribute to and maintain more efficient, effective, and high-performing government operations.
- Reducing the organization's risk exposures.

Institutionalizing Practice Examples

- Internal audit charter includes the nature of the assurance services provided to the organization.
- Documented audit programs and procedures.
- Internal audit procedures manual.
- Internal audit training on performance/value-for-money auditing.

---

[16] Such audits are process-based and the objectives could relate to the effectiveness and adequacy of governance, risk management, and control processes of the subject of the engagement or be more focused; that is to say, auditing the performance management systems based on authoritative auditing standards or assessing the quality of performance information or performance reports.

Services and Role of Internal Auditing

Level 3 – Integrated

Advisory Services

Purpose — To analyze a situation and/or provide guidance and advice to management. Advisory services[17] add value without the internal auditor assuming management responsibility. Advisory services are those that are directed toward facilitation rather than assurance and include training, systems development reviews, performance and control self-assessment, counseling, and advice.

Essential Activities
- Include in the internal audit charter the authority to perform advisory services and the types of advisory services expected by the organization.
- Develop appropriate policies and procedures for conducting advisory services.
- Ensure that the CAE retains the prerogative of establishing the appropriate audit techniques and procedures for performing the advisory engagement and the right of reporting to senior management when the nature and materiality or results pose significant risks to the organization.
- Implement practices to ensure that the independence and objectivity of internal auditors conducting the engagement are not impaired, and if so, ensure that appropriate disclosure is made.
- Ensure that internal auditors exercise due professional care in conducting advisory-service engagements.
- With respect to each individual advisory service:
  o Determine the methodology and type of advisory service; e.g., will it be combined with an assurance engagement or be performed separately?
  o Communicate to management and obtain agreement on the principles and approach that the IA activity will employ in performing and reporting on the advisory service.
  o Obtain assurance that management will be responsible for decisions and/or actions taken as a result of advice provided through advisory services.
  o Perform the advisory service.
  o Communicate the results of the advisory service.

Outputs
- Provision of guidance or advice to management with respect to governance, risk management and/or controls, including soft controls.

Outcomes
- Influencing change to improve the organization's operations and results achieved.
- Added value by management acting on the results of advisory services or through such "partnering" relationships.

Institutionalizing Practice Examples
- Senior management support for the conduct of advisory services by the IA activity.
- Internal audit charter includes the authority to perform advisory services and the types of advisory services.
- Documented guidelines for the performance of advisory services.
- Internal audit training on relevant types of advisory services.

---

[17] These services are referred to as "Consulting Services" in the Definition of Internal Auditing found in the International Professional Practices Framework. The *Standards* include implementation standards relating to consulting services.

Services and Role of Internal Auditing

Level 4 – Managed

Overall Assurance on Governance, Risk Management, and Control

Purpose — To conduct sufficient work to provide an opinion on the overall adequacy and effectiveness of the organization's governance, risk management, and control processes. The IA activity has coordinated its audit services to be sufficiently comprehensive that it can provide reasonable assurance at a corporate level that these processes are adequate and functioning as intended to meet the organization's objectives.

Essential Activities

- Include the authority to express an organization-wide opinion in the internal audit charter.
- Ensure that the scope of the IA activity encompasses the whole of the organization's governance, risk management, and control processes.
- In accordance with its risk-based audit plan, review sufficient elements of the governance, risk management, and control processes to express an opinion on an organization-wide basis.
- Support the overall opinion with audits conducted over a specific period of time (usually annually).
- Express an opinion for each individual audit engagement performed during the specific period of time.
- Support the opinions with sufficient and competent audit evidence gathered in accordance with the *Standards*.
- Perform an annual corporate governance audit, if necessary, to support the overall opinion.
- Perform an annual enterprise-wide risk management audit, if necessary, to support the overall opinion.
- Use technology-enabled auditing and analytics (including continuous auditing, data analysis, and the use of computer-assisted audit tools [CAATs]) to help provide independent objective assurance over the adequacy and effectiveness of governance, risk management, and internal control processes.
- Attest to the reasonableness of management's assertion or representation (if available) on the effectiveness of its governance, risk management, and control processes in supporting the achievement of objectives by:
  - o Reviewing the adequacy and results of management's monitoring activities.
  - o Assessing the transparency, fairness, and consistency of management's conclusions with respect to the results.
- Drawing upon management's monitoring results, internal audit's own risk assessments and audit activities, and results of relevant assessments performed by other assurance providers, provide an independent opinion on the overall effectiveness of governance, risk management, and control processes in supporting achievement of objectives.[18]
- Communicate the overall opinion and what it means to senior management, including concepts such as "reasonable assurance" and "positive" or "negative" assurance opinion.
- Reinforce the notion that overall responsibility for effective governance, risk management, and control processes over operations, compliance, and financial reporting rests with management.

Outputs

- Internal audit expresses an opinion on whether the organization's governance, risk management, and control processes are effective in providing reasonable assurance that the organization's objectives are met.

---

[18] For more information, see Sam Huibers, *Combined Assurance: One Language, One Voice, One View* (Lake Mary, FL: The Institute of Internal Auditors Research Foundation), 2016.

Outcomes

- Board and stakeholder confidence that the organization's governance, risk management, and control processes are adequate and functioning as intended to meet the organization's objectives.
- Board and relevant stakeholders are able to deliver on their corporate governance obligations.
- Assurance processes are integrated and aligned so that senior management and the board obtain a comprehensive, holistic view of the effectiveness of their organization's governance, risks, and controls to enable them to set priorities and take any necessary actions.
- Knowledge acquired by the IA activity is used by the organization to strengthen its governance, risk management, and control processes.

Institutionalizing Practice Examples

- Senior management support for the IA activity's role in providing an organization-wide opinion.
- Internal audit charter includes the authority to express an organization-wide opinion.
- Guidance on providing overall assurance on governance, risk management, and control.
- Risk-based audit and services plan.
- Internal audit training relevant to auditing governance, risk management, and control processes.
- IA activity's knowledge management program includes standard formalized tools/resource library.
- Organization's annual statement of internal control.

Services and Role of Internal Auditing

Level 5 – Optimizing
Internal Audit Recognized as Key Agent of Change

Purpose — To have sufficiently developed the professional and leadership capacity of the IA activity to provide foresight and serve as a catalyst to achieve positive change in the organization.

Essential Activities

- Update the internal audit charter to include any expanded roles and scope of the IA activity (e.g., provision of insight into the reasons for its conclusions, foresight into the implications for the organization, and serving as a positive change agent within the organization).
- Use leading industry and technological practices and innovative approaches in internal auditing.
- Focus the IA activity's strategy on continuous customer service.
- Augment the personal skills and knowledge of the internal audit professionals in cutting-edge areas of technology, business processes, industry-specific practices, and implications of a changing business environment.
- Look outside the organization to monitor the changing business environment and its impact on the organization's business, governance, risk management, and control processes.
- Facilitate corporate learning on the effects and impacts of the changing environment on the organization's governance, risk management, and control processes.
- Contribute to the development and implementation of enterprise risk management strategies in the organization.
- Contribute to enhancing the organization's risk and control environment through supporting management improve its first and second lines of defense functions and risk mitigation.
- Provide advice on entity-wide issues and emerging trends.
- Communicate how internal audit results contribute to improved business processes and the organization's strategic objectives.

Outputs

- The IA activity provides full assurance and advisory services, including audit coverage in the areas of governance, entity-level controls, risk management, fraud, new strategic initiatives, programs, or business practices as needed by the organization.
- Enterprise risk management is an integral part of the strategic agenda of the IA activity.
- The IA activity's strategy is focused on innovation, client service, and value delivery.
- The IA activity positions itself as a key player by contributing to the organization's vision through its responsiveness to both internal and external needs.

Outcomes

- The organization accepts and uses the business knowledge of internal auditors to improve business processes and help meet strategic objectives.
- The IA activity is recognized as influencing positive change and continuous improvement to business processes, bottom-line results, and accountability within the organization.
- IA activity is recognized as a trusted advisor and is sought out for its insight and foresight.
- The work of the IA activity adds higher value by influencing organizational policy and contributing to better decisions by key stakeholders.

Institutionalizing Practice Examples

- Senior management support for internal audit's key role in influencing change in the organization.
- IA activity publishes periodic "audit intelligence" reports or briefs to share its insights on how emerging issues affect the organization and the achievement of organizational objectives.
- Internal audit charter includes any expanded roles and scope of the IA activity.
- Internal audit strategy document.
- Internal audit training and professional development program.

People Management

Level 2 – Infrastructure
Skilled People Identified and Recruited

Purpose — To identify and attract people with the necessary competencies and relevant skills to carry out the work of the IA activity. Appropriately qualified and recruited internal auditors are more likely to provide credibility to the internal audit results.

Essential Activities
- Identify and define the specific audit tasks to be conducted.
- Identify the knowledge, skills (technical and behavioral), and other competencies required to conduct audit tasks.
- Develop job descriptions for positions.
- Determine proper pay classification for positions.
- Conduct valid, credible[19] recruitment process to select appropriate candidates.

Outputs
- Internal audit positions are filled with appropriately qualified persons.

Outcomes
- Audit work is conducted with proficiency and due professional care.
- There are credible audit observations, conclusions, and recommendations.

Institutionalizing Practice Examples
- Visible commitment and support through senior management action to ensure that a competent and qualified CAE is in place and the necessary resources are provided to appropriately staff the IA activity.
- Staffing and recruitment policy.
- Job descriptions.
- Classification system, including levels specific to internal auditing.

---

[19] In this context, "valid, credible" means fair, open, transparent, and under the control of the CAE. The recruitment process used by the IA activity relates specifically to its level of independence because a fundamental element of the independence of the IA activity relies on the individual auditor's impartial, unbiased attitude and lack of personal impairments to objectivity. Accordingly, the CAE must be free to recruit and place internal auditors based on their qualifications. If the organization's management or elected officials assign persons to an IA activity, these actions can impair both the independence and the credibility of the IA activity.

People Management

Level 2 – Infrastructure

Individual Professional Development

Purpose — To ensure that internal auditors continuously maintain and enhance their professional capabilities.

Essential Activities

- Determine a target number of staff training hours/days/credits for each individual consistent with prescribed auditing standards or relevant certifications.
- Identify the training courses, providers, or sources that would be sufficient to accomplish valid professional development.
- Encourage individuals to be members of professional associations.
- Track and document training hours/days, course types, and providers to monitor compliance with personal training requirements and to support continuous professional development.
- Develop periodic reports to document training accomplished by each internal auditor.

Outputs

- Individual certificates of attendance at relevant training sessions.
- Periodic reports of types and amounts of training achieved by each internal auditor.

Outcomes

- Assurance that all persons carrying out functions of the IA activity maintain the minimum level of continuous learning required by auditing standards, professional certifications, or organizational policy.
- Individual commitment to life-long learning.[20]

Institutionalizing Practice Examples

- Visible commitment and support through senior management action to provide suitable resources to facilitate individual professional development.
- Personal training and professional development plan.
- Training budget.
- Training provider/course register.

---

[20] For more information, see James Rose, *Mapping Your Career: Competencies Necessary for Internal Audit Excellence* (Lake Mary, FL: The Institute of Internal Auditors Research Foundation, 2016).

People Management

Level 3 – Integrated

Workforce Coordination

Purpose — To coordinate the development of the periodic audit and services plan to the human resource levels authorized to the IA activity. Because resources are often constrained, the IA activity needs to use appropriate methods to set priorities on planned projects and services to limit its commitments to a "doable" quantity and type of projects and services.

Essential Activities
- Estimate the quantity and scope of audit and other services that would be required to complete the IA activity's proposed work plan.
- Compare required resources to the quantity and scope of work that could be produced by the existing staff complement (based on number and expertise level of internal auditors available).
- Use prioritization "filters"[21] to link the audit activity's periodic work-plan projects, commitments, and assignments to the maximum internal audit staff capacity (both for number and expertise of staff).
- Consider other resourcing strategies (e.g., recruitment, co-sourcing, outsourcing, etc.), as necessary, when the internal audit capacity is not sufficient in the IA activity.

Outputs
- A periodic audit and services plan that represents full utilization of budgeted/authorized resources available to complete the work plan.[22]

Outcomes
- Resources to carry out the periodic audit and services plan.
- Organizational continuation of the IA activity's base human resource levels to discharge its responsibilities from year to year.

Institutionalizing Practice Examples
- Senior management support for the necessary resources to implement the periodic audit and services plan.
- Organizational policy on workforce coordination.
- Formal periodic (annual or multiyear) planning process.
- Training.

---

[21] Prioritization filters are the criteria used to rank audits in order of priority. For instance, when audit projects on the proposed periodic work plan exceed the number of staff hours available, what means are used to determine the priority of specific projects in order to reduce the number/scope of proposed projects to those which the IA activity is capable of carrying out? These criteria may include "management interest," "extent of problems already occurring," or other risk factors. In addition, prioritization filters may involve decisions about how a proposed project will be conducted. For example, if engineering expertise were required by a potential audit but not available in audit staff, should the IA activity outsource the specialization or defer the audit until internal staffing can be carried out?

[22] Learning how to "budget" and coordinate the periodic audit and services plan to the existing capacity and capabilities of internal audit staff provides the "stepping stone" skill that audit managers need to begin the higher-level process of basing human resource proposals on the organization's risk profile and the IA activity's role in supporting/assisting/participating in the organization's risk management function.

People Management

Level 3 – Integrated
Professionally Qualified Staff

Purpose — To staff the IA activity with professionally qualified staff and retain the individuals who have demonstrated a minimum level of competence.

Essential Activities

- Create a competency framework (career progression of positions and responsibilities from entry level to manager) to support professional growth and development, taking into consideration the organization's environment and specific knowledge and skills (technical, behavioral, and industry-specific) required.[23]
- Establish explicit, objective criteria (expectations) for evaluating performance of staff at each level of the competency framework.
- Routinely/periodically compare each staff member's performance against the expectations for their present position and discuss with the staff member.
- Create a "training and development plan" for each individual to guide improvement and progress through the competency framework.
- Establish programs to ensure that auditors obtain their CIA and/or other appropriate professional designations (including CGAP, CFSA, CCSA, CRMA, QIAL, CFE, CISA, CPA, CA, etc.) as well as industry-specific certifications, if relevant.
- Fund incentives (or salary increments) for satisfactory and/or excellent performance within each level.
- Encourage involvement in relevant professional associations.
- Determine the mix of skills and levels of staff needed and assess whether they can be developed internally or must be obtained through co-sourcing or outsourcing.

Outputs

- Qualified experienced people in all positions, whether internal, co-sourced, or outsourced.
- Systematic performance appraisal process resulting in periodic appraisals is applied equitably and fairly to each staff member.
- Career movement for staff who demonstrably exhibit desired professional development.
- By investing in certification and continuing professional development, internal auditors stay abreast with the latest developments, skills, and new technologies.

Outcomes

- Fair and transparent means for progressing from entry level to managerial levels within the IA activity.
- Opportunities for staff to match their personal goals with the professional qualifications needed by the IA activity and the organization.
- The IA activity demonstrates its commitment to growth, development, and improvement through systematic and ongoing mentoring, training, and education for all staff members.
- Improved communication and analytical/critical thinking skills through a mix of deliberate training programs and on-the-job feedback and coaching.
- Internal auditing is considered a career.

---

[23] For more information, see *The IIA Global Internal Audit Competency Framework*, 2013, and the IIA Practice Guide "Talent Management: Recruiting, Developing, Motivating, and Retaining Great Team Members" (Lake Mary, FL: The Institute of Internal Auditors, 2015).

Institutionalizing Practice Examples

- Senior management support for the resources and action necessary to recruit and retain professionally qualified staff.
- Human resource strategies and policies (e.g., staff retention strategy and policy, training and professional development strategy and policy).
- Internal audit competency framework.
- Master training and development plan and individual training and professional development plans (based on personal and project needs).
- Professional certifications and/or training days required by legislation.
- Annual audit engagement performance appraisal systems.
- Formal incentive and recognition program.
- Rotational/internship programs.

People Management

Level 3 – Integrated

Team Building and Competency

Purpose — To develop staff members' capacity to function effectively in a team environment, beginning with focus on the individual project team. Because many public sector audits cover scopes that require the concerted effort of a team of auditors to conduct, and because the skills needed to conduct an audit are not necessarily the same skills to work effectively in a group environment, additional team competencies are required.

Essential Activities
- Introduce communication and coordination mechanisms to support team building (e.g., periodic team meetings, shared team data resources, and agreed-upon project assignments and schedules).
- Develop criteria for effective teamwork behaviors and practices and incorporate the criteria into the staff competency framework.
- Provide professional development opportunities on topics such as teamwork and team leadership, effective communication, and relationship building.
- Identify and assign team leadership role to selected individuals, with explicit duties, responsibilities, and authority.
- Implement team-based rewards for successful accomplishments to reinforce desired team behaviors.
- Develop team members to assume changing roles as the organization changes.

Outputs
- Audits and other projects are carried out by one or more groups of individuals (self-directed and integrated work teams) working together productively.

Outcomes
- The IA activity is able to handle larger scope projects.
- Staff are given more opportunities for personal and professional development in the areas of communication, leadership, and relationship building.
- Project quality can be improved by sharing the knowledge, experience, and perspectives of several individuals.

Institutionalizing Practice Examples
- Internal audit competency framework.
- Training on topics such as teamwork and team leadership, effective communication, and relationship building.
- Team communication strategies (e.g., team-backs and shared resources).
- Mentoring program.
- Workplace and home balance program (flexible working arrangements such as job sharing and flexible work weeks).
- Incentive and recognition program.

People Management

Level 4 – Managed
Workforce Planning

Purpose — To coordinate workforce activities to achieve current business needs of the IA activity. Workforce planning involves developing a workforce plan that sets out the resources, skills, training, and tools required to conduct the audits that have been identified (or are proposed) in the periodic audit and services plan.

Essential Activities
- Identify the resources, skills, training, and tools needed to address areas of greatest significance and risk to the organization (which have been identified in risk-based audit planning).
- Link identified skills to the competency framework (career progression system).
- Quantify workforce requirements in terms of number of resources and skillsets required to allow internal audit to carry out its activities.
- Compare the required skills (including specialized skills such as information technology, fraud, etc.) to an inventory of those in place/on staff within the IA activity.
- Analyze the gap between existing resource levels and the desired competencies.
- Develop and implement strategies for closing the resource gap, including training, tools development, rotational or guest auditor programs, co-sourcing, and outsourcing.
- Communicate to management and other key stakeholders the priorities and strategies of the IA activity, particularly if it will not be able to carry out the entire periodic audit and services plan.

Outputs
- A staffing plan that identifies resources needed and strategies to be used to provide sufficient capacity to complete the periodic audit and services plan.

Outcomes
- Sufficient capacity (in skills, staffing numbers, and tools) to meet the proposed/established periodic audit and services plan.
- Organizational acceptance of resources needed for the IA activity to discharge its responsibilities.

Institutionalizing Practice Examples
- Senior management support for the capacity and resources needed for the IA activity to discharge its responsibilities.
- Organizational policy requiring workforce planning.
- Legislation requiring workforce planning.
- Talent management plan.
- Succession plan.

People Management

Level 4 – Managed
IA Activity Supports Professional Bodies

Purpose — To provide leadership and professional development opportunities for the internal audit staff by supporting their involvement and participation in professional bodies.

Essential Activities
- Identify relevant professional bodies whose activities, advocacy efforts, and professional themes are congruent with the IA activity's current and long-term professional development goals or with the organization's strategies or operations.
- Establish mechanisms and criteria for the IA activity's support of staff time and participation in professional body activities (financial, time, and other resources).
- Track or encourage reporting of professional involvement by staff to link professional contributions to their advancement in the career development process within the organization.
- Use the knowledge acquired to strengthen staff capacity and the IA activity.

Outputs
- Recognition for individual staff members as leaders or contributors to professional body activities.
- Performance reporting of the IA activity's contributions to the profession.

Outcomes
- Personal and professional development of individual audit staff members through opportunities to share, collaborate, and learn from others outside their employer organization.
- Currency of audit staff members with recent developments and their profession's evolutionary growth.
- Recognition by the organization of the leadership role of its IA activity in relevant fields.

Institutionalizing Practice Examples
- Senior management support for staff involvement in professional bodies.
- Performance appraisal and a career development system.

People Management

Level 4 – Managed

Internal Audit Contributes to Management Development

Purpose — To integrate the development of the organization's managers with the training and experiences of the IA activity and vice versa. The organization and the IA activity pursue a strategy to encourage people with a good understanding of governance, risk management, and controls to work and contribute throughout the organization.

Essential Activities
- Identify the specific processes or functions of the IA activity that generate knowledge, skills, or experiences that are valued by the organization.
- Identify the specific functions and processes within the organization (e.g., business activities, information technology, etc.) where the IA activity would benefit through training and development.
- Develop mechanisms appropriate to the organization to expose candidates to these processes or functions.
- Identify candidates both within the IA activity and within the organization who would benefit from professional development and exposure to governance, risk management, internal control concepts, and other identified processes and functions.
- Promote the IA activity as a means for managers to develop broad knowledge of governance, risk management, and control concepts as well as of the organization's business processes.
- Market the IA activity as an ambassador promoting the importance of good governance, risk management, and control processes.

Outputs
- Completed "training" exposure to internal audit culture and knowledge by individual candidates.
- Managers working throughout the organization who understand governance, risk management, and control principles and processes.
- Internal auditors with improved business acumen, and a greater knowledge of business strategies and processes who can leverage business relationships to add value to the organization and increase the organization's confidence in the IA activity.

Outcomes
- Future business leaders, who embody the organizational culture and values, understand the control environment, and understand the impact of internal audit on the organization.
- Strengthened and harmonized organization-wide understanding of governance, risk management, and control principles and processes.
- The IA activity is seen as a resource for education, counsel, and recommendations for improvement.

Institutionalizing Practice Examples
- Senior management support for the IA activity directly contributing to management development.
- Rotation policy between the IA activity and the rest of the organization (e.g., management's recruiting of internal audit staff for vacant management-level positions or recruiting management-level staff to spend specified periods in the IA activity before assignment to other positions).
- Guest auditor program.
- Organization-wide internal audit education program.
- Participation of management and operational staff in internal audit training opportunities.
- Participation of management and operational staff as audit team members.
- Control self-assessment.

People Management

Level 5 – Optimizing
Workforce Projection

Purpose — To coordinate long-term workforce development activities to meet future business needs of the IA activity. Workforce projection involves developing a strategic workforce plan that sets out the IA activity's objectives for competency development and workforce activities, in conjunction with the organization's projected strategic needs, and developing plans to guide workforce development activities for the IA activity.

Essential Activities
- Project the IA activity's future services and required skills/resources in the context of the organization's strategic plans.
- Analyze and develop the workforce requirements needed by the IA activity (in terms of number of resources and skillsets) to carry out the projected services.
- Analyze the gap between existing and desired resources and competencies.
- Develop long-term strategies for closing the resource gap (e.g., training and development of existing staff, creation of new positions, reclassifying existing positions, reorganizing reporting relationships, developing consulting relationships, engaging technological tools, co-sourcing, and outsourcing).

Outputs
- Workforce plan for staff or position development to ensure that adequate competencies are in place in the IA activity for future work needs.
- Proposal (as needed) to strengthen the capacity of the IA activity through addition or modification of staff skills and experience, co-sourcing, outsourcing, etc.

Outcomes
- Organizational recognition of the relationship between its strategic objectives and risks and the makeup of its IA activity.
- Recognition of the IA activity's long-term relevance and capacity to provide value-added services.

Institutionalizing Practice Examples
- Senior management support for workforce projection development activities.
- Organizational policy on strategic workforce planning.
- Internal audit strategic competency plan process.[24]
- Internal audit strategic plan.
- Internal audit strategic staffing plan.

---

[24] For more information, see the IIA Practice Guide "Creating an Internal Audit Competency Process for the Public Sector" (Lake Mary, FL: The Institute of Internal Auditors, February 2015).

People Management

Level 5 – Optimizing
Leadership Involvement with Professional Bodies

Purpose — To facilitate and support top leaders of the IA activity becoming key leaders within relevant professional bodies. In addition to making contributions to the profession through their volunteer work, the CAE and other internal auditors will become thought leaders and influence the growth and evolution of the profession. Participating in the administration and/or leadership of professional bodies helps auditors learn and practice higher-level people skills, since their roles vis-à-vis their colleagues require different means of interacting from their "auditor" or "manager" role within their own organization.

Essential Activities
- Establish a supportive culture for leadership involvement and contribution to professional bodies.
- Recognize accomplishments of internal audit leadership in relevant professional bodies.
- Learn from other IA activities and their organizations and integrate relevant strategic thinking and practices within the IA activity and the organization.
- Use the knowledge acquired to contribute to improved learning strategies for the organization.

Outputs
- Offices held at leadership levels of relevant professional bodies.
- Projects completed that contribute significantly to the advancement of the profession.

Outcomes
- Development and refinement of leadership and management skills along with the professional savvy of internal auditors.
- Organizational influence over the development and direction of the profession.
- Continuous learning from involvement with other professionals and their environments.
- The IA activity is outward looking and strategic in its thinking.

Institutionalizing Practice Examples
- Senior management support for leadership involvement with professional bodies.
- Actively positioning people to become key leaders of professional bodies.

Professional Practices

Level 2 – Infrastructure

Audit Plan Based on Management/Stakeholder Priorities

Purpose — To develop periodic (annual or multiyear) plans for which audits and/or other services will be provided, based on consultations with management and/or other stakeholders.

Essential Activities
- Identify all auditable entities in the organization and document the audit universe.
- In collaboration with senior management and/or other stakeholders, determine the time period to be covered by the plan (i.e., annual, multiyear, or a combination).
- Through consultations with senior management and/or other stakeholders (e.g., senior government officials or external auditor), identify the areas/issues that are considered as priorities to be addressed by the IA activity.
- Identify the audit engagements, including cyclical audits, to be included in the plan and what other services the IA activity will be providing to the organization.
- Determine the indicative audit objectives and scope for each audit engagement and those for any other services, if applicable.
- Determine the overall resources required (human, financial, material) to accomplish the plan by including the sum of resources for each audit engagement, other services to be provided, and any additional resources that may be required to respond to other management and/or stakeholders priorities that might arise during the period covered by the plan.
- Determine the mix of human resource capabilities required to accomplish the plan (from within the IA activity or through co-sourcing or outsourcing).
- Obtain senior management's and/or the board's approval of the plan and the resources required to implement the plan.

Outputs
- A periodic (annual or multiyear) internal audit and services plan based on priorities identified by senior management within the organization and/or other key stakeholders.

Outcomes
- Understanding by the IA activity of management's and/or other stakeholders' priorities.
- Opportunities identified by the IA activity to improve organizational objectives and operations.

Institutionalizing Practice Examples
- Visible commitment and support through senior management action to identify the areas/issues that are considered as priorities to be addressed by the IA activity, and approval of the periodic internal audit plan along with the resources required to implement the plan.
- Formal internal audit planning process.
- Documented audit universe.

Professional Practices

Level 2 – Infrastructure

Professional Practices and Processes Framework

Purpose — To help facilitate the performance of audit engagements—with the independence and objectivity and proficiency and due professional care—envisaged in the internal audit charter and the Mission of Internal Audit, the Definition of Internal Auditing, the Code of Ethics, the Core Principles, and the *Standards*.[25] The professional practices and processes framework includes the policies, processes, and procedures that will guide the IA activity in managing its operations; developing its internal audit work program; and planning, performing, and reporting on the results of internal audits.

Essential Activities

- Recognize the mandatory nature of the Definition of Internal Auditing, the Code of Ethics, the Core Principles, and the *Standards* in the internal audit charter.
- Develop relevant policies for the IA activity (e.g., human resources, information management, and financial).[26]
- Develop overall guidance for preparing the internal audit work program.
- Document the actual processes for preparing the work program.
- Document the actual processes for planning, performing, and reporting on the results of individual audit engagements, including communication with management.
- Develop standard methodology, procedures, and tools (including information technology tools) to be used by the IA activity for planning, performing, and reporting on the results of the audit engagement, including working paper guidelines.
- Implement the processes necessary to assure the quality of the individual audit engagements.
- Establish and maintain a system to monitor the disposition of results communicated to management (e.g., a follow-up process to ensure management actions have been effectively implemented or management has accepted the risk of not taking action).

Outputs

- Professional practices manual for the IA activity.
- Standardized guidance, methodology, approaches, and repeatable and sustained processes.

Outcomes

- Audit engagements are performed with proficiency and due professional care.
- Demonstrated consistency in the work of the IA activity and conformance with professional practices and standards.

Institutionalizing Practice Examples

- Visible commitment and action by senior management through supporting the professional nature of internal auditing and providing appropriate resources to create a professional practices and processes framework.
- Internal audit charter recognizes the mandatory nature of the Definition of Internal Auditing, the Code of Ethics, the Core Principles, and the *Standards*.
- Documented internal audit policies, processes, procedures, and methodology.
- Internal audit professional practices manual.
- Internal quality assurance processes, including supervisory review and sign-off of working papers.

---

[25] The Definition of Internal Auditing, the Code of Ethics, the Core Principles, and the *Standards* are considered mandatory guidance and are included in the International Professional Practices Framework promulgated by The IIA.

[26] The form and content of the policies and procedures are dependent upon the size and structure of the IA activity and the complexity of its work.

Professional Practices

Level 3 – Integrated
Risk-Based Audit Plans

Purpose — To systematically assess risks and focus the priorities of the IA activity's periodic audit and services plan on risk exposures throughout the organization.

Essential Activities

- Consult with senior management and the board to understand their perception of environmental and organizational risks.
- Consider the organization's risk management framework, if established.
- Understand the organization's strategic goals and objectives in order to appropriately align the audit and services plan to them.
- Conduct the internal audit periodic risk assessment by:
  - o Updating the audit universe.
  - o Identifying the audit entities where exposure to risk is highest.
  - o Determining the likelihood that the identified risk could become a significant or pervasive deficiency impacting on the achievement of the audit entity's objectives.
  - o Identifying the risk responses put in place or actions taken by management to address or manage such risks.
  - o Identifying the need for additional or different risk responses.
  - o Including an assessment of fraud indicators.
- Include as audit engagements in the periodic audit and services plan those audit entities where risk exposure to the organization is high and/or management risk responses are not considered appropriate.
- Obtain senior management and/or board approval of the plan.
- Review and adjust the plan, as necessary, in response to changes in the organization's business, risks, operations, programs, systems, and controls.

Outputs

- A periodic internal audit and services plan based on risk exposures throughout the organization and revised as necessary to address emerging risks.
- Communication of risk and control information to appropriate parties within the organization.

Outcomes

- Understanding the organization's risks and opportunities and contributing to management's mitigation of them, thereby improving overall risk management and control systems.

Institutionalizing Practice Examples

- Senior management support for a risk-based audit plan based on the IA activity's periodic risk assessment.
- Documented procedures for conducting the periodic risk assessment.
- Training on risk-based audit planning.

Professional Practices

Level 3 – Integrated
Quality Management Framework

Purpose — To establish and maintain processes to continuously monitor, assess, and improve the effectiveness of the IA activity. Processes include ongoing internal monitoring of the performance of the IA activity as well as periodic internal and external quality assessments.

Essential Activities

- Develop policies, practices, and procedures, including those leveraged through information technology, that contribute to the continuous improvement of the IA activity.
- Develop and document the roles, responsibilities, and accountabilities for performing, reviewing, and approving the internal audit work products at each stage of the audit engagement process.
- Implement and maintain a quality assurance and improvement program, which includes ongoing internal monitoring as well as periodic internal and external quality assessments.[27]
- Develop systems and procedures to monitor and report on the quality assurance and improvement program.
- Develop systems and procedures to monitor and report on the performance and effectiveness of the IA activity, including:
  - o Achievement of the Definition of Internal Auditing, demonstration of the Core Principles, and conformance with the Code of Ethics and the *Standards*.
  - o Adequacy of the internal audit charter, objectives, policies, and procedures.
  - o Appropriateness of the IA activity's reporting relationship.
  - o Contribution to the organization's governance, risk management, and control processes.
  - o Compliance with applicable laws, regulations, and government or industry standards.
  - o Effectiveness of continuous improvement activities and adoption of leading practices.
  - o Whether the IA activity adds value and improves the organization's operations.
- Develop systems and processes to follow up implementation of recommendations made to improve the effectiveness and performance of the IA activity and its conformance with the *Standards*.

Outputs

- A quality management framework (established processes, systems, and procedures, including those supported by information technology) with which all operations of the IA activity should conform.
- Follow-up actions by the IA activity to ensure implementation of recommendations to achieve improvements and conformance with the *Standards*.
- Clear roles, responsibilities, and accountabilities for the IA activity.

Outcomes

- Reasonable assurance that processes and products of the IA activity achieve the Definition of Internal Auditing, conform with the *Standards,* the Code of Ethics, and relevant legal requirements, and demonstrate the Core Principles.
- Increased stakeholder confidence by documenting the IA activity's commitment to quality and successful practices.

---

[27] For more information, see the IIA Practice Guide "Quality Assurance and Improvement Program" (Lake Mary, FL: The Institute of Internal Auditors, March 2012).

Institutionalizing Practice Examples

- Formal internal audit strategy.
- Internal audit professional practices manual.
- Technology-supported audit operations (e.g., working paper storage, data analytics, report writing).
- Internal quality assessments or self-assessments.
- External quality assurance reviews.
- Regulatory assessments.
- Peer reviews.
- Stakeholder surveys.
- External audit feedback.

Professional Practices

Level 4 – Managed

Audit Strategy Leverages Organization's Management of Risk

Purpose — To link the IA activity's periodic audit and services plan with the organization's enterprise risk management strategies and practices.[28]

Essential Activities

- Understand the organization's enterprise risk management strategies and practices through consultation with management and key stakeholders and review of relevant documentation, internal and external to the organization.
- Translate the organization's risk management strategies into operational terms; consider external influences, such as the organization's overall environment (e.g., legislation or culture) and key stakeholders' needs, and internal influences, such as management priorities, business processes, and the organization's operations.
- Leverage the organization's enterprise risk management strategy and design and implement an enterprise-wide risk and vulnerability assessment process for internal audit planning.
- Include in the internal audit and services plan those areas identified as high risk by management, if appropriate, and those identified by the IA activity through its risk and vulnerability assessment.
- Continually monitor the organization's risk profile and revise the internal audit and services plan, if necessary, and obtain senior management and/or board approval.
- Focus on strategic risks as well as operational, financial, and compliance risks during the conduct of audit engagements.
- Perform a periodic enterprise-wide risk management audit.

Outputs

- The IA activity has developed a framework that encompasses risk and control considerations at all levels of the organization's governance, risk management, and control processes.
- An IA activity periodic audit and services plan that leverages the organization's enterprise risk management strategies and practices.
- An IA activity periodic audit and services plan where the audit coverage is aligned with the organization's major business and operational initiatives and risks, and anticipates emerging issues and risks.

Outcomes

- The IA activity leverages its work using key business risks identified through the organization's enterprise risk management processes, recognizing that the audit universe should fully address the organization's major risks and cover all its operations.
- The IA activity contributes to enterprise risk management by supporting the organization's identification of risks, understanding its risk appetite and risk-mitigation strategies, ensuring risks are integrated and aggregated, and making appropriate recommendations.

Institutionalizing Practice Examples

- Enterprise risk management strategy and practices in place within the organization.
- Ongoing discussion between the CAE and senior management on the implication of risks facing the organization and to obtain the CAE's insights on risk.
- Senior management support for the alignment between the IA activity's periodic audit and services plan with the organization's enterprise risk management strategies and practices.
- IA activity participates on key and critical management and operational committees.

---

[28] Enterprise risk management strategies and practices refers to formal and documented processes put in place by the organization to identify, assess, manage, and control potential events or situations to provide reasonable assurance regarding the achievement of the organization's objectives.

Professional Practices

Level 5 – Optimizing

Strategic Internal Audit Planning

Purpose — To understand the organization's strategic directions and emerging issues and risks, and change the IA activity's skillsets and audit services to meet potential future needs.

Essential Activities

- Keep abreast of the organization's external and internal environment (including the strategic, business, legal, and compliance risks of the organization) to identify and assess emerging trends, issues, and risks.
- Work closely with senior management to understand the organization's current and future strategic directions.
- Provide management and the board with insight as to the implications of emerging trends, issues, and risks.
- Conduct a comprehensive assessment to identify gaps in practices, tools, and skillsets that need to be addressed to respond to current and emerging issues and risks to the organization.
- Assess options to address the gaps, such as revised or additional procedures, practices, and/or tools (including information technology tools), additional and/or different staff, co-sourcing, or outsourcing arrangements.
- Ensure that all internal auditors follow a rigorous continuing education and professional development program.
- Review the periodic internal audit and services plan on a real-time basis and make appropriate revisions, as necessary, to align it with changing organizational strategies and risks; obtain senior management and/or board approval.

Outputs

- A flexible audit approach and dynamic audit and services plan that aligns with the organization's strategic directions and addresses emerging and potential issues and risks.
- An internal audit specific strategy that meets stakeholder expectations and drives internal audit initiatives.

Outcomes

- The IA activity has achieved organization-wide respect for demonstrating value in anticipating the organization's needs and contributing to the achievement of strategic and organizational objectives.
- Knowledge acquired from looking at the external environment is incorporated into internal audit strategic and operational planning.
- Changes within organizational governance, management and culture are factored into the IA activity's periodic strategic planning processes and its approach to service delivery.

Institutionalizing Practice Examples

- Strategic planning process in place within the organization.
- Senior management commitment to support internal audit's contribution to the achievement of strategic and organizational objectives through strategic internal audit planning.
- Formal internal audit strategic plan.[29]
- IA activity participates on top-level strategic management committees.
- Ongoing assessment of the IA activity identifying strengths, weaknesses, gaps, and constraints (e.g., SWOT analysis).
- Training and professional development plans.

---

[29] For more information, see the IIA Practice Guide "Developing the Internal Audit Strategic Plan" (Lake Mary, FL: The Institute of Internal Auditors, July 2012).

Professional Practices

Level 5 – Optimizing

Continuous Improvement in Professional Practices

Purpose — To integrate the performance data, global leading practices, and feedback received from ongoing quality assurance and improvement program processes to continuously strengthen and develop the IA activity's capacity to deliver world-class internal auditing.

Essential Activities

- Review and update the IA activity's charter, policies, practices, and procedures on a regular basis to ensure that they reflect those of world-class auditing activities (e.g., including audit innovation, technology-enabled auditing and analytic capabilities, etc.).
- Implement recommendations resulting from the ongoing quality assurance and improvement program to support world-class internal auditing.
- Monitor the IA activity's performance management system to assess results and take action to optimize performance.
- Implement information technology solutions to optimally enable the IA activity's operations and results.
- Monitor and augment the IA activity's knowledge management program to support world-class auditing.
- Contribute to relevant professional associations to learn about and apply global leading practices to the IA activity.
- Share leading practices, performance improvements, and emerging global trends with the organization's senior management to garner support for continuous improvement within both the IA activity and the organization.

Outputs

- The IA activity demonstrates innovative internal audit professional practices to achieve the Definition of Internal Auditing, conform with the Code of Ethics and the *Standards,* demonstrate the Core Principles, assure its organizational independence and objectivity in its work approach, and comply with applicable laws, regulations, and government and/or industry specific standards through reliable and valid reporting.
- The IA activity's charter, policies, and operations reflect world-class auditing.
- Information technology is optimally aligned to enable audit operations and results.

Outcomes

- The IA activity contributes significantly to the organization's governance, risk management, and control processes and adds value and improves the organization's operations.
- The IA activity is strategic and outward looking in its thinking and practices continuous learning.
- The IA activity is viewed as an integral business partner within the organization and respected as a source of business intelligence with a clear understanding of the risks and challenges the organization faces in achieving its goals.

Institutionalizing Practice Examples

- Senior management's visible support for continuous improvement of internal audit professional practices.
- Internal audit charter provides for the conduct of world-class audit activities.
- Quality assurance and improvement program.
- Performance management system.
- Knowledge management program.
- Global benchmarking with world-class internal audit activities.
- Attendance at global professional forums.

Performance Management and Accountability

Level 2 – Infrastructure

Internal Audit Business Plan

Purpose — To establish a periodic plan for delivering the services of the IA activity, including administrative and support services, and the expected results.

Essential Activities
- Identify the internal audit vision and overall strategy to achieve that vision.
- In line with the overall strategy, determine the business objectives of and results to be achieved by the IA activity, taking into consideration the periodic/annual audit and services plan.
- Determine the administrative and support services required for effective delivery of the IA activity (e.g., human, material, and information technology).
- Prepare any relevant schedules and determine the resources needed to achieve the established objectives.
- Develop the necessary business plan to meet those objectives.
- Obtain senior management and/or board approval of the business plan.

Outputs
- A business plan that identifies the activities to be carried out over the relevant period, including all the resources required.

Outcomes
- The plan provides a basis for controlling operations and holding internal audit managers accountable for their use of resources to achieve the IA activity's business objectives.

Institutionalizing Practice Examples
- Visible commitment and support through senior management action to provide the resources necessary to implement the internal audit business plan.
- Organizational policy requiring business plans.
- Separate operating budget for the IA activity.

Performance Management and Accountability

Level 2 – Infrastructure

Internal Audit Operating Budget

Purpose — To be allocated and use its own operating budget to plan the services of the IA activity.

Essential Activities
- Establish a realistic budget for the activities and resources identified in the IA activity's business plan, considering both fixed and variable costs.
- Develop budgeting standards that align with the rest of the organization.
- Obtain senior management and/or board approval of the operating budget.
- Review the budget on an ongoing basis to ensure that it remains realistic and accurate, identifying and reporting any variances.

Outputs
- An operating budget that reflects the financial cost of implementing and executing the IA activity's business plan.
- An operating budget that is approved by the organization's senior management and/or board.

Outcomes
- The IA activity can allocate approved resources according to the needs identified in its business and operational plans.
- Strengthened accountability within the organization.
- Assurance that the IA activity is compliant with authorities and that its assets are safeguarded.

Institutionalizing Practice Examples
- Visible commitment and support through senior management action to approve an appropriate internal audit operating budget.
- Structured organizational budgetary system and processes.
- Periodic internal audit business plan.

Performance Management and Accountability

Level 3 – Integrated

Internal Audit Management Reports

Purpose — To receive and use information to manage the IA activity's day-to-day operations, support decision-making, and demonstrate accountability.

Essential Activities
- Identify internal audit management reporting needs and requirements.
- Develop relevant data collection mechanisms.
- Design reports to meet the needs of users and key stakeholders.
- Provide internal audit management with relevant information and reports on a timely and periodic basis.
- Provide internal audit stakeholders with relevant information and reports on a timely and periodic basis.
- Monitor the use of management information and reports for continued relevance and revise, as required.

Outputs
- A range of information management reports produced and provided on a timely and periodic basis that contains accurate, relevant, reliable, and credible information that internal audit management needs to discharge its management responsibilities and accountabilities.

Outcomes
- Internal audit management responsibilities and accountabilities are discharged appropriately.

Institutionalizing Practice Examples
- Senior management's commitment to manage and account for results.
- Organizational policy requiring management's accountability for results.
- Project management system.

Performance Management and Accountability

Level 3 – Integrated

Cost Information

Purpose — To provide sufficient information from the financial tracking system such that the IA activity understands the cost information sufficiently to use it to manage its services as economically and efficiently as possible. This practice goes slightly beyond budget variances and integrates the relationship of outputs to inputs.

Essential Activities

- Develop accurate information on the service costs of the IA activity.
- Employ a cost management system to capture costs throughout the service delivery process.
- Align cost management systems with the organization's financial and operational systems and its financial and management reporting practices.
- Monitor actual costs against established expected or standard costs at various stages of delivery.
- Monitor the cost management system on a regular basis, ensuring that the cost structure remains relevant and that cost information is produced/obtained in the most efficient and cost-effective way.
- Report on the utilization of resources, cost overruns, and cost savings.
- Utilize cost information in decision-making and management of the IA activity's operations.

Outputs

- Costing systems.
- Information on the cost of the internal audit services and activities.
- Cost analysis that can be used to support management's decisions.

Outcomes

- Cost information can be used to control costs of the IA activity's programs/services, support decision-making, and set user fees for cost recovery, if relevant.

Institutionalizing Practice Examples

- Organizational financial tracking and cost system and processes.
- Time recording and reporting system.
- Training on cost management and analysis.

Performance Management and Accountability

Level 3 – Integrated
Performance Measures

Purpose — In addition to cost data, to develop meaningful indicators and measures that enable the IA activity to measure and report on its performance and routinely monitor its progress against targets to ensure that results are achieved as economically and efficiently as possible. These will be primarily input and process measures, with some output or qualitative outcome measures.[30]

Essential Activities

- Identify the IA activity's business and organizational objectives.
- Determine what internal audit operations need to be measured.
- Document the performance management system, identifying:
    - o Performance data to be collected.
    - o The frequency of data collection.
    - o Who is responsible for data collection.
    - o Data quality control.
    - o Who generates performance data reports.
    - o Who receives the reports.
- Develop performance measures (input/output ratios, productivity measures).
- Establish performance targets.
- Use the performance information to monitor the IA activity's operations and results against established objectives and take appropriate action.
- Report on the IA activity's performance to senior management and/or relevant stakeholders, as required (e.g., quarterly/annual reports on the IA activity).
- Evaluate periodically the cost effectiveness, currency, and relevance of the performance measures.

Outputs

- A framework for measuring the IA activity's performance, including meaningful indicators and measures of performance.
- Consistent monitoring processes and a performance reporting regime for the IA activity.
- Data that provide meaningful information on the IA activity's performance.
- Periodic reports to senior management and/or the board.

Outcomes

- An understanding and demonstration of how day-to-day operations work toward the achievement of the IA activity's business and organizational objectives.
- Internal audit management is able to use the performance information to monitor operations and results against established objectives, make informed decisions, and demonstrate accountability.

---

[30] Fundamental metrics will likely be in place—these relate to measurable internal audit activities (e.g., input: resources/ working days available and used; output: number of reports produced, recommendations made, percentage of completion of the audit and services plan; outcome: impact of recommendations implemented such as dollars saved or additional revenue collected, client satisfaction). For more information, see the IIA Practice Guide "Measuring Internal Audit Effectiveness and Efficiency" (Lake Mary, FL: The Institute of Internal Auditors, December 2010).

Institutionalizing Practice Examples

- Organizational policy requiring monitoring and reporting on the achievement of business and organizational objectives.
- Organizational policy requiring management's accountability for results (e.g., accountability agreements).
- Time information recording and reporting system.
- Balanced scorecard.
- Client satisfaction survey.

Performance Management and Accountability

Level 4 – Managed

Integration of Qualitative and Quantitative Performance Measures

Purpose — To enable the IA activity to use information on performance to measure and monitor fluctuations that affect its results. The activity has balanced its use of quantitative and qualitative data to help it achieve its strategic objectives.

Essential Activities

- Clearly identify the strategic objectives of the IA activity.
- Consider the organization's strategic and operational objectives and risk appetite when establishing the objectives to be achieved by the IA activity.
- Develop comprehensive performance measures and targets that establish a level of acceptable risk, cost, quality, and results.
- Develop systems to monitor and measure performance.
- Use information on performance to measure and monitor fluctuations that affect the results of the IA activity.
- Use information on performance to optimize the use of internal audit resources to address the organization's risk exposures.
- Obtain input from key stakeholders on a regular basis on the effectiveness and quality of the IA activity.
- Incorporate the results of the quality assurance and improvement program, which includes ongoing monitoring and periodic internal and external assessments, with those of the performance management system and use the information to improve performance, as appropriate.
- Monitor the implementation of the IA activity's recommendations by management to assess the impact on and value added to the organization (e.g., more effective operations and improved governance, risk management, and control processes).

Outputs

- Performance measures exist that cover stakeholder satisfaction, internal audit processes and results (risk assessment/audit planning; performing the audits; reporting and value-added), and innovation and capabilities (training, technology, knowledge of business).
- Conclusions as to the quality of ongoing performance of the IA activity.

Outcomes

- Full integration of qualitative and quantitative measures to ensure that the strategic objectives of the IA activity have been met and value has been added.[31]
- Performance metrics reinforce the IA activity's relevance to key stakeholders, enhance accountability, and foster a culture of continuous improvement.

Institutionalizing Practice Examples

- Senior management support for using quantitative and qualitative data to help achieve strategic objectives.
- Internal audit quality assurance and improvement program.
- System/processes in place to follow up disposition of internal audit results and assess the impact on and value added to the organization.
- Internal audit periodic planning and reporting process that uses quantitative and qualitative performance information.

---

[31] For more information, see Jane Seago, *Delivering on the Promise: Measuring Internal Audit Value and Performance* (Lake Mary, FL: The Institute of Internal Auditors Research Foundation, 2016).

- Financial measures such as cost savings, improved efficiencies, or other monetary benefits related to organizational objectives.
- Client satisfaction surveys.
- Surveys of key stakeholders.
- Independent assessment of IA activity's performance in meeting key stakeholders' expectations.

Performance Management and Accountability

Level 5 – Optimizing

Outcome Performance and Value to the Organization Achieved

Purpose — To report on the effectiveness of the IA activity to demonstrate transparency and accountability to the organization's stakeholders and the public, and identify the contribution and impact made by the IA activity with the resources provided.

Essential Activities

- Establish impact measures that identify the value produced from the IA activity's efficiently and effectively aligned people, processes, and technology.
- Collect the relevant data.
- Identify organizational-level impact of the IA activity, including:
  - o Risks mitigated.
  - o Cost-saving opportunities.
  - o Financial recovery opportunities.
  - o Improvements to the governance, risk management, and control processes of the organization.
  - o Value added to the organization as a result of assurances provided to senior management and/or the board.
- Report to internal and external stakeholders on the effectiveness of the IA activity and to the public, if appropriate.
- Obtain and use feedback from external stakeholders to improve the effectiveness of the IA activity.

Outputs

A report that describes substantively the contribution and impact made by the IA activity and demonstrates its value to the organization.

Outcomes

- The IA activity demonstrates that it, like other parts of the organization, is responsible for contributing to the organization's success and performance and is held accountable for results.
- The IA activity's value-added contribution to improving the organization's governance, risk management, and control processes is demonstrated.
- The significance of the benefit provided by the IA activity's contribution to organizational objectives is demonstrated.
- Citizens are engaged and the public more clearly understands the distinct and different roles and responsibilities that internal audit and management have in meeting organizational objectives.
- External stakeholders have timely and relevant performance information to make appropriate decisions.

Institutionalizing Practice Examples

- Visible senior management support and commitment to report on the effectiveness of internal audit to the public.
- Organization's annual/periodic report to the public.
- IA activity's periodic report on achievements.
- System to follow up on impacts from implementing internal audit recommendations.
- Performance measurement system, including specific indicators on the IA activity's contribution to and impact on the organization.
- Client surveys.
- Formal assessment of the results achieved by the IA activity by the audit committee, senior management, and other partners.

Organizational Relationships and Culture

Level 2 – Infrastructure
Managing within the IA Activity

Purpose — To focus the management effort of the IA activity on its own operations and relationships within the activity itself, such as organizational structure, people management, budget preparation and monitoring, annual planning, providing the necessary audit tools and technology, and performing audits. Interactions with organizational managers are focused on carrying out the business of the IA activity.

Essential Activities
- Determine and formally establish the appropriate organizational structure within the IA activity.
- Identify the roles and responsibilities of the key positions in the IA activity.
- Support the IA activity's organizational needs and the reporting relationships of the persons within the activity.
- Assess the requirements for and obtain the necessary resources and audit tools, including technology-based tools, needed to both manage and carry out the work of the IA activity.
- Manage, direct, and communicate within the IA activity.
- Foster relationships and encourage ongoing and constructive communication within the IA activity.

Outputs
- An appropriate organizational structure within the IA activity that is consistent with the organization's needs and culture.
- Audit and technology-based tools needed to carry out the work of the IA activity.
- Effective interpersonal relationships and communication within the IA activity.

Outcomes
- Effectively managed and functioning IA activity that adds value to the organization.

Institutionalizing Practice Examples
- Visible commitment and support through senior management action to establish a separate organizational entity for the IA activity, ensure that a competent and qualified CAE is in place, and provide the necessary resources.
- Formally approved organizational structure.
- Job descriptions for positions in the IA activity.
- Operating budget for the IA activity.

Organizational Relationships and Culture

Level 3 – Integrated

Integral Component of Management Team

Purpose – To participate in the organization's management activities in some form as a valued member of the management team. Although the CAE does not carry out management's responsibilities, the CAE is included in communications and forums of the management team, and as an observer, is able to maintain a channel of communication with senior management.

Essential Activities

- The CAE keeps abreast of management priorities and changing business processes and new initiatives within the organization.
- Senior management shares the organization's key management plans and information reports with the CAE (e.g., strategic and business plans and financial reports).
- The CAE shares key organizational management plans and issues with the staff of the IA activity.
- The CAE participates and contributes, as appropriate, on key management committees/forums as part of the organization's management team.
- The CAE encourages internal audit staff involvement in key organizational committees, as appropriate.
- Senior management is consulted and contributes to the development of internal audit plans.
- Information concerning the plans and activities of the IA activity is regularly exchanged with senior management.
- The IA activity liaises with and coordinates the external auditors' work on behalf of management.

Outputs

- The CAE and other senior managers in the IA activity participate with the organization's management at key management events (committees, forums) and receive all relevant management-related communications. Participation and attendance at management forums provide an opportunity for the CAE to be apprised of strategic and operational developments and to raise high-level risk, systems, procedures, and control-type issues at an early stage.

Outcomes

- The IA activity's leaders are seen as integral (fundamental) to the organization's management team and contribute to achieving organizational results.

Institutionalizing Practice Examples

- Senior management visibly supports and demonstrates through its actions that the CAE is a valued member of the management team.
- Internal audit charter includes the CAE's role as part of the management team.
- Organizational policy formally includes the CAE as a member of the organization's management team.
- The CAE is part of the organization's management distribution list that includes all of the organization's key decisions.
- Formal briefing package/presentations for senior management on the IA activity.

Organizational Relationships and Culture

Level 3 – Integrated

Coordination with Other Review Groups

Purpose — To share information and coordinate activities with other internal and external providers of assurance and advisory services to ensure appropriate organizational coverage and minimize duplication of effort.

Essential Activities

- Identify the relevant external and internal providers of assurance and advisory services for the organization (including those risk and control functions in the first and second lines of defense within the organization).
- Identify areas where sharing plans, information, and results of activities may be beneficial.
- Develop processes/mechanisms to share information and communicate and coordinate on issues of mutual concern.
- Establish a consistent process for the basis of reliance, where the IA activity considers reliance on the work of other assurance and advisory service providers.[32]
- Liaise regularly with the organization's external auditor to share plans and encourage complementarity of the work of the IA activity with that of the external auditor.

Outputs

- Process/mechanism to share information and communicate and coordinate on issues of mutual concern.
- Consistent process for the basis of reliance on the work of other assurance and advisory service providers.

Outcomes

- Optimizing the relationship and minimizing duplication of effort between the IA activity and other providers of assurance and advisory services.
- Reducing inefficiencies, saving costs, increasing the level of assurance, and leveraging subject-matter expertise through collaboration between the IA activity and other risk and control functions within the organization (including those in the first and second lines of defense).

Institutionalizing Practice Examples

- Senior management supports sharing information and coordinating the work of the IA activity with that of other internal and external providers of assurance and advisory services, while appreciating the critical role that internal audit has in providing independent and objective assurance services to the organization.
- Regular meetings/forum with relevant providers of assurance and advisory services.
- Formal protocol/coordination document between the IA activity and the external auditor to govern the various components of a successful relationship and make it sustainable.

---

[32] For more information, see The IIA Practice Guide "Reliance by Internal Audit on Other Assurance Providers" (Lake Mary, FL: The Institute of Internal Auditors, December 2011).

Organizational Relationships and Culture

Level 4 – Managed

CAE Advises and Influences Top-level Management

Purpose — To facilitate the organization's understanding and appreciation of the vision, leadership, and foresight of the CAE, and to develop a professional relationship with top-level management that fosters frank exchanges while maintaining independence and objectivity. Senior management values the CAE for advice on strategic issues.

Essential Activities

- The CAE regularly communicates and interacts directly with top-level management.
- The CAE contributes as part of the management team, advising on emerging business and strategic issues.
- The CAE understands stakeholders' expectations and communicates risks in the context of strategic business goals and objectives.
- The CAE fosters collaboration and trust between internal auditors and organizational management on relevant internal audit and organizational issues.
- The CAE shares knowledge on best-practice business processes with operational managers throughout the organization.
- The CAE sets a strong example of effective, ethical, and insightful management that is demonstrated by the advice and guidance given to others.
- The CAE supports top-level management by developing a formal, transparent, and cooperative relationship with the external auditor and encourages reliance by the external auditor on internal audit's work.

Outputs

- Clear, concise, forthright, relevant, and timely communication with top-level management.
- Specific issues/special requests from top-level management for the CAE to address informally and/or formally.

Outcomes

- The IA activity can clearly articulate its strategic and shorter-term goals and the value it delivers to the organization.
- The IA activity's vision is consistent with that of the organization and aligned with key stakeholders.
- The IA activity's leadership is respected for vision and foresight.
- Top-level management trusts and values the advice of the CAE and the IA activity.

Institutionalizing Practice Examples

- Senior management supports the relationships and mechanisms established to facilitate the provision of advice from the CAE to top-level management.
- Formal reporting relationship.
- Formal process/mechanism put in place to ensure regular and direct communication and interaction with top-level management.
- Regular in-camera sessions with top-level management.
- Feedback mechanisms for the IA activity (e.g., client surveys).
- Communication sessions (e.g., "town-hall meetings") among internal auditors and operational management.
- Communication strategy with the external auditor (e.g., attendance at audit committee meetings and formal presentations on external audit strategy and key risks).

Organizational Relationships and Culture

Level 5 – Optimizing
Effective and Ongoing Relationships

Purpose — To use strong relationship management skills of the CAE for maintaining appropriate visibility and alignment with key stakeholders, management, and audit committee needs and expectations.

Essential Activities
- Proactively communicate key strategic and operational issues to management and other key stakeholders and make recommendations.
- Participate on or be an observer at all of the organization's mission-critical committees.
- Facilitate organizational learning by identifying changes in the global business environment that impact the organization.
- Consistently link all services of the IA activity to its vision, values, and strategic objectives.
- Continually share knowledge about the organizational strategy and business initiatives within the IA activity.
- Maintain and foster the mutually respectful and professional relationship with the organization's external auditor.
- Contribute to optimizing audit committee effectiveness (e.g., refinement of its charter, committee member training, etc.).
- Lead in supporting management's harmonization of the organization's risk and control functions (e.g., first and second lines of defense).

Outputs
- A process/mechanism for regular interaction/briefings with key stakeholders, management, and audit committee members.
- An internal audit communication plan that identifies communication needs of key stakeholders, management and the audit committee.
- A stakeholder relationship management plan that sets out the key IA activities to respond to the needs of the stakeholders.

Outcomes
- Key stakeholders, management, and audit committee members understand and value internal audit.
- IA activity is seen as a strategic and trusted advisor and is sought out for advice and insight.
- The IA activity is seen as a credible business partner throughout the organization.
- The IA activity's vision and values are consistent with those of the organization and aligned with key stakeholders.
- The IA activity plays a key role in development of the "tone from the top."
- The IA activity is seen as responsive to the needs of its key stakeholders.
- The external auditor relies on the work of the IA activity.

Institutionalizing Practice Examples
- Visible commitment and support from senior management to foster such ongoing relationships.
- Internal audit charter includes a formal process/mechanism for regular interaction and communication with and feedback from management, key stakeholders, and audit committee members.
- Internal audit communication plan.
- Internal audit stakeholder relationship management plan.

Governance Structures

Level 2 – Infrastructure
Reporting Relationships Established

Purpose — To establish formal reporting relationships (administrative and functional[33]) for the IA activity.

Essential Activities
- Develop an internal audit charter or other document that formally defines the purpose, authority, and responsibility of the IA activity.
- Ensure that senior management and/or the board (governing body), if applicable, formally approves the charter.
- Adopt a mission and/or vision statement for the IA activity.
- Communicate the purpose, authority, and responsibility of the IA activity throughout the organization.
- Ensure that the CAE reports administratively and functionally to a level within the organization that allows the IA activity to fulfill its responsibilities.
- Review and update the charter on a regular basis and obtain senior management and/or board approval.

Outputs
- The IA activity has a defined charter.
- The administrative and functional reporting relationships for the IA activity have been formally established.

Outcomes
- The IA activity has a formal mandate.
- The reporting relationship/organizational placement of the IA activity is sufficient to prevent the organization from interfering with internal audit's ability to determine its scope, perform its work, and communicate its results.
- The documented purpose, authority, and responsibility define the role of internal audit and provide a basis for management and/or the board (governing body) to evaluate the operations of the IA activity.

Institutionalizing Practice Examples
- Visible commitment and support through senior management action to establish an IA activity and identify formal reporting relationships.
- Legislation providing a legal basis for internal audit.
- Formally approved internal audit charter.
- Formal and approved internal audit organization structure.
- Communication strategy to educate and promote the importance of internal auditing.

---

[33] The functional reporting line for the IA activity is the ultimate source of its independence and authority. IIA Standard 1110 – Organizational Independence requires that the CAE report to a level within the organization that allows the internal audit activity to fulfill its responsibilities. The chief audit executive must confirm to the board, at least annually, the organizational independence of the internal audit activity.

Organizational independence is effectively achieved when the CAE reports functionally to the board. Generally, the CAE also has an administrative or "dotted" reporting line to a member of senior management. To enhance stature and credibility, The IIA recommends that the CAE report administratively to the chief executive officer (CEO) so that the CAE is clearly in a senior position, with the authority to perform duties unimpeded. [Standard 1100 and Implementation Guide 1110 (2016)].

Governance Structures

Level 2 – Infrastructure

Full Access to the Organization's Information, Assets, and People

Purpose — To provide the authority for the IA activity to obtain access to all the information, assets, and people that it requires to carry out its duties.

Essential Activities

- Include in the internal audit charter the authority for the IA activity to obtain access to all the organization's information, assets, and people it requires to carry out its duties.
- Establish a policy relating to the specific authority of the IA activity with respect to full, free, and unrestricted access to the organization's records, physical properties, and personnel relative to any of the organization's operations being audited.
- Establish procedures to formally access such records, physical properties, and personnel relative to any of the organization's operations being audited.
- Establish procedures to follow up when client management chooses not to disclose documents needed during the performance of an internal audit engagement.

Outputs

- Policies and procedures providing the authority and means of accessing the information, assets, and people that the IA activity needs to effectively carry out its work.

Outcomes

- Unrestricted access for the IA activity.
- The capacity of the IA activity to carry out its audit work without interference and scope limitations.

Institutionalizing Practice Examples

- Senior management communicates and actively demonstrates its support for full access.
- Internal audit charter that includes a provision for full access.
- Organizational policy and procedures relating to internal audit's full access.
- Communication strategy to ensure policy is promulgated and understood.

Governance Structures

Level 3 – Integrated
Funding Mechanisms

Purpose — To establish a robust and transparent funding process that ensures adequate resources to allow the IA activity to discharge its obligations.[34]

Essential Activities
- Determine the resources needed to effectively carry out the IA activity.
- Include as resources all funding required to support the IA activity in delivering the assurance and advisory services needed to address the risks identified (including administrative and support services).
- Establish a process/mechanism to approve the IA activity's resource needs that is transparent and sufficiently independent of management influence.
- Identify the impact of resource limitations and communicate the impact to senior management and/or the board.

Outputs
- A robust and transparent funding process is established for the IA activity which is sufficiently independent of management influence.

Outcomes
- Sufficient funding is available to effectively carry out the IA activity.
- The budget allocated to the IA activity considers the risks and impacts of not auditing.

Institutionalizing Practice Examples
- Senior management support to ensure that a funding mechanism is in place that does not impair internal audit's independence.
- Formal and documented process for resource allocation to the IA activity.
- Process and funding is tied to the internal audit risk-based plan.

---

[34] Budgetary controls and considerations imposed by administrative reporting lines should not impede the ability of the IA activity to accomplish its mission.

Governance Structures

Level 3 – Integrated

Management Oversight and Support of the IA Activity

Purpose — To establish a mechanism/process within the organization to provide oversight and advice to the IA activity, review its results, and ensure appropriate actions are taken to strengthen its independence. Operating managers respect audit independence, are responsive to audit requests, and provide constructive feedback to facilitate the audit process. Involvement of a variety of managers in the decisions related to the IA activity helps to extend the activity's support and scope beyond a single individual and ensure its independence.

Essential Activities

- Recommend and contribute to the establishment of the appropriate mechanism/process to provide oversight and advice.
- If a committee of senior managers is that mechanism, contribute by recommending membership attributes, assisting in the development of its charter, and providing secretariat support.
- Establish policies and procedures for the IA activity to communicate, interact, and report to the committee of senior managers.
- Meet regularly with senior managers to increase management's awareness about governance, risk assessment, internal audit, and the value of a strong control environment.
- Encourage senior managers' support for the independence of the IA activity through their advocacy efforts, such as communicating the IA activity's mandate, authority, independence, and benefits throughout the organization.
- Encourage senior management support for rotational programs to help address IA activity skill gaps and increase the number of ambassadors for internal audit within the organization.
- Coordinate the work of the IA activity and share relevant results and information with other assurance and advisory service providers for the organization.
- Working with management, champion the implementation and coordination of an effective Three Lines of Defense model within the organization to facilitate an understanding of its importance, the respective roles and responsibilities of the various risk and control functions, and to minimize duplication or gaps in risk and control coverage.[35]

Outputs

- A mechanism/process within the organization to provide oversight and advice, and review the results of the IA activity.
- Policies and procedures for the IA activity to communicate, interact, and report to the committee of senior managers or other mechanism/process.
- Processes to coordinate and share relevant results of the work of the IA activity and that of other assurance and advisory service providers.
- Processes to identify and coordinate the work of the various risk and control functions in the organization's three lines of defense.

---

[35] For more information, see the IIA Practice Guide "Internal Audit and the Second Line of Defense" (Lake Mary, FL: The Institute of Internal Auditors), January 2016.

Outcomes

- The independence, objectivity, and effectiveness of the IA activity are strengthened.
- The value of internal audit is demonstrated through senior management's support of internal audit's contribution and impacts.
- Senior management shares in the accountability for the effectiveness of the IA activity.
- Issues with organizational relationships are mitigated by senior management.
- Work among assurance and advisory service providers for the organization is coordinated, resulting in less duplication of effort and appropriate organizational coverage.
- The roles and responsibilities of the three lines of defense are understood, coordinated, and effective.

Institutionalizing Practice Examples

- Senior management support to establish an appropriate mechanism to provide oversight and advice to the IA activity.
- Legislation requiring an oversight committee.
- Internal audit charter includes reference to internal audit oversight mechanism/process.
- Organizational policies and procedures relating to internal audit oversight.
- Management oversight committee.
- Regular meetings/forums of assurance and advisory service providers.

Governance Structures

Level 3 – Integrated

CAE Reports to Top-Level Authority

Purpose — To strengthen the CAE's independence by establishing a direct functional reporting relationship to the governing body and a direct administrative reporting relationship to either the chief executive officer (CEO) or governing body.[36]

Essential Activities
- Reflect in the internal audit charter the direct functional reporting relationship of the CAE to the governing body and the direct administrative reporting relationship to either the CEO or the governing body.
- Ensure that the CAE meets regularly and communicates directly, as necessary, with the governing body and CEO, if applicable.

Outputs
- The CAE's reporting relationship provides for a direct link and regular reporting to the governing body and CEO, if applicable.

Outcomes
- An optimal reporting relationship is established that solidifies the independence of the CAE.
- The reporting relationship provides organizational independence for the IA activity.
- The reporting relationship enables the IA activity to provide valued and trusted advice to the governing body and CEO.

Institutionalizing Practice Examples
- Senior management commitment to support a functional reporting relationship to the governing body and a direct administrative reporting relationship to either the CEO or governing body.
- Legislation establishing a legal basis for the reporting relationships.
- Internal audit charter identifying the reporting relationships.
- Organizational policy identifying the reporting relationships.
- Standardized/periodic meeting schedule with governing body/CEO.

---

[36] According to the Glossary of the *Standards* (January 2017), the definition of Board is "The highest level of governing body (e.g., a board of directors, a supervisory board, or a board of governors or trustees) charged with the responsibility to direct and/or oversee the organization's activities and hold senior management accountable. Although governance arrangements vary among jurisdictions and sectors, typically the board includes members who are not part of management. If a board does not exist, the word "board" in the *Standards* refers to a group or person charged with governance of the organization. Furthermore, "board" in the *Standards* may refer to a committee or another body to which the governing body has delegated certain functions (e.g., an audit committee)."

Governance Structures

Level 4 – Managed
Independent Oversight of the IA Activity

Purpose — To establish an oversight body, including members independent of the organization's management, to assure the independence of the IA activity, broaden the activity's scope of input and influence, and help to strengthen the organization's accountability.

Essential Activities
- Contribute to the establishment and performance of the independent oversight body by recommending membership attributes, assisting in the development of its charter, providing secretariat support, and influencing the agenda.[37]
- Align the charter of the oversight body with that of the IA activity to reinforce the critical relationship between the oversight body and the IA activity.
- Establish policies and procedures for the IA activity to communicate, interact with, and report to the independent oversight body (including assurance that the CAE has direct access to the chair of the oversight body, if necessary).
- Establish the role of the oversight body with respect to appointment, performance evaluation, and removal, where necessary, of the CAE.[38]

Outputs
- An oversight body (including members independent of management) that provides oversight and functional direction to the IA activity.
- Policies and procedures for the IA activity to communicate, interact with, and report to the independent oversight body.
- The authority of the IA activity is visibly and actively supported by the independent oversight body.
- CAE attends independent oversight body meetings, as required.

Outcomes
- The independence of the IA activity is assured and the activity's scope of input and influence is broadened.
- Accountability within the organization is strengthened.
- The IA activity meets the needs of the oversight body and other significant stakeholders resulting in improved stakeholder support for internal audit.
- The oversight body is seen as exemplary (e.g., sets and adheres to its own charter and follows the organization's code of ethics; oversees and evaluates the responsibilities of management, the IA activity, and the external auditors).

Institutionalizing Practice Examples
- Senior management support to establish the infrastructure necessary for the oversight body (e.g., resources, secretariat).
- Legislation requiring an independent oversight body.
- Internal audit charter includes reference to independent internal audit oversight.
- Organizational policies and procedures relating to independent oversight of the IA activity.
- Audit oversight committee with members independent of the organization's management.
- Formal recruitment processes and orientation/training for audit committee members.
- Annual audit committee self-assessment.

---

[37] For more information, see "Independent Audit Committees in Public Sector Organizations," IIA Global Public Sector Insight (Lake Mary, FL: The Institute of Internal Auditors, June 2014).

[38] For more information, see IIA Practice Guide "Chief Audit Executives Appointment, Performance Evaluation, and Termination" (Lake Mary, FL: The Institute of Internal Auditors, 2010).

Governance Structures

Level 5 – Optimizing
Independence, Power, and Authority of the IA Activity

Purpose — To fully actualize the IA activity's independence, power, and authority.

Essential Activities
- Confirm, garner support, and formally approve/sanction the appropriate mandate for the IA activity.
- Communicate the independence, power, and authority of the IA activity throughout the organization, to its stakeholders, and to the public.
- Explore and assess leading internal audit practices in other jurisdictions to enhance the independence and objectivity of the IA activity.
- Tailor and apply leading practices external to the organization to improve the governance, risk management, and control processes within the organization, including the means by which the oversight body discharges its responsibilities.

Outputs
- The full independence, power, and authority of the IA activity are formally concretized (e.g., through legislation, legal mandate, management, and oversight body support).
- The words and actions of senior management, the oversight body, and all key stakeholders demonstrate full acceptance for and support of the IA activity.

Outcomes
- The IA activity is not a discretionary policy of management.
- The IA activity has uncompromising independence, power, and authority in determining the scope of internal auditing, performing its work, and communicating its results.
- The IA activity has full organizational independence.
- The organization's culture clearly recognizes and accepts the value of internal audit.
- Government and organizational consensus exists on the role of internal audit.

Institutionalizing Practice Examples
- Visible support by senior management for continuous improvement of internal audit, including enhancing its breadth and scope.
- Strategic information and communication strategy advocating the independence, power, and authority of internal audit.
- Benchmarking key success factors for IA activities globally (e.g., legislation, audit committee mandate, internal audit charter, organizational policy).

Annex B: Examples Using the IA-CM

The IA-CM has been applied globally to improve the effectiveness of internal auditing. It has been used to assess the capability level of individual IA activities as well as support the improvement of internal auditing on a country-wide basis.

It has been used for self-assessment and continuous improvement of the IA activity, capacity development of internal auditors, strategic planning, visioning and communication, and benchmarking. It has also been applied for the purposes of performing Internal Assessments (Standard 1311) as part of an IA activity's Quality Assurance and Improvement Program.

This Annex includes some examples of current uses of the IA-CM. Examples highlighted include IA activities from Asia, Africa, North America, South America, and Europe and range from mature to less mature functions and from governments using the model to a one-person shop in the United States.

B.1 Self-Assessment, Continuous Improvement, and Capacity Development

B.1.1 The IIA Netherlands

The IIA Netherlands used the IA-CM as a starting point and developed an Internal Audit Ambition Model (IAAM), which was published in June 2016.

The Introduction to the model states:

"As the Internal Audit Capability Model for the Public Sector (IA-CM) was already a proven methodology which illustrates the levels and stages through which an internal audit (IA) activity can evolve as it defines, implements, measures, controls, and improves its processes and practices, we used this model as a starting point."

The Overview further states that "our main considerations on using this model [IA-CM] were:

First, the IA-CM has been internationally validated and is a proven model. Second, its guidelines are sufficiently general to be applied to both the private and public sector. And third, the maturity levels are in line with generally accepted models such as the Capability Maturity Model Integration (CMMI)."

The Introduction continues, as follows:

"However, the IIA and LIO felt a Dutch application of the IA-CM was needed to align it with the current state of internal auditing in the Netherlands. First, the IA-CM was published in 2009 and the internal audit profession and the world it operates in has developed significantly. Second, the IA-CM had been developed for the public sector specifically and a broader scope was desired for the Netherlands also given the fact that most Dutch companies have two-tier boards.

"Furthermore, both the CQA and the Dutch CAEs felt the need to link the existing IA-CM with the IPPF and the standard of the Dutch Chartered Accountants NV COS 6101.

"Our work consisted of validating the guidelines from the IA-CM with a broad group of CAEs, matching the guidelines with the IPPF, NBA standards and updating the IA-CM based on the recent publications of IIA

Global, the Internal Audit Foundation and IIA Netherlands and the IFAC Code of Ethics (which is the basis for the codes of ethics of the IIA and NBA). Additional input was gathered from best practices developed by a variety of internal audit professionals.

"To align the name of this new model with the intended use of the model, we renamed this new model the "IA AM." This IA AM is intended for self-assessment, formulating the role, scope and ambition level of the IAF in consultation with the Supervisory Board. It is also a tool for capacity building and increasing awareness of the IAF and the internal audit profession in general among our stakeholders. Its primary users are expected to be internal audit professionals together with the profession's stakeholders. In line with the principle-based nature of internal auditing, this model is not intended to be prescriptive in terms of how a process should be carried out. More important is that the user assesses whether their internal audit activity is organized to realize their ambition level.

"As an ambition model the IA AM is not a static document and needs to be reviewed on a regular basis. Just as the world around us changes at exponential speed, we as an internal audit profession need to adapt to these changes. The ambitions of today are not the same as we will have tomorrow if we want to provide continuous insight, assurance and advice.

"Therefore, this is the start of a broad professional dialogue amongst auditors with the ambition to improve this model over the next few years. We would like internal auditors to use this tool and share their experiences and assessments for national benchmark research in order to gain insight in the current level of quality and in the ambition level of IAFs."

The IA AM can be obtained by contacting IIA Netherlands.

B.1.2 Government of the Republic of Indonesia

The Government of Indonesia (GoI) is committed to improving internal audit capabilities in the public sector.

Recognizing the value of the IA-CM, in 2010, the Badan Pengawasan Keuangan dan Pembangunan (BPKP, the GoI's internal audit institution) used the IA-CM to carry out an assessment survey of the strengths and weaknesses of all GoI's Inspectorates General (IGs). This was one of several initiatives that BPKP has undertaken and is undertaking to encourage IGs to upgrade their skills, capacity and capability. This is further to Presidential Instruction no. 4/2011 to support and ensure that IGs play a significant forward role in governance and oversight.

By way of background, BPKP constitutes the Government of Indonesia's Internal Auditor, and is responsible to the President of Indonesia.

BPKP is directed by a chairman who supervises the secretary and five deputies, heads of its 33 Regional Representative Offices, heads of its centers, and the Inspectorate. Deputies' portfolios consist of specific sectors: Economy Affairs; Politic, Social, and Security Affairs; Local Government Finance; State Accountant; and Investigations. BPKP has over 6000 employees, almost 4000 of whom are functional auditors.

BPKP carries out the duties and functions mandated to it by legislation namely, the internal control functions assigned to it by the Presidential Regulation of the Republic of Indonesia No. 192 of 2014 on Badan Pengawasan Keuangan dan Pembangunan and Presidential Instruction No. 9 of 2014, and Government Regulation No. 60

of 2008. The duties and authority of the BPKP are also set out in Presidential Decree No. 4 of 2011, Law No. 30 of 2002, and Law No. 20 of 1997.

Article 44 of Presidential Regulation No. 192 of 2014, states that "The BPKP Head shall be appointed and removed by the President."

BPKP's current roles, responsibilities and authority are identified in Article 2 in the Presidential Regulation No. 192 0f 2014, which describes the specific functions that BPKP has in its duty of conducting governmental affairs in the field of supervising state/local finances and national development.

To complement its legislative mandate, BPKP has formulated and adopted the following vision and mission.[39]

The Vision: "To be a World-Class Government Internal Auditor to Improve Accountability in National Financial Management and Development."

BPKP's mission statement is as follows:

1) Conducting Internal Control over Financial Management and National Development Accountability to Support Clean and Effective State and Public Sector Corporation Governance;

2) Fostering the implementation of an effective Government Internal Control System; and

3) Developing the capability of the Government Internal Auditor to be professional and competent.

"Government Internal Auditor refers to the position of BPKP as an official government internal control agency that is directly responsible to the President. ...In the interests of the President, BPKP also serves as a strategic partner of Heads of State Institutions and Local Government Chief Executives in terms of providing consultancy services. ...It is expected that the information generated by the BPKP internal control processes/operations will be objective, impartial and free from interference by third parties who would seek to undermine the principle of independence.[40]

In addition, Article 3 of Presidential Regulation no. 192 of 2014 identifies functions for which BPKP is responsible on a government-wide basis, including:

"...j.   Developing government internal audit capabilities and encouraging a certification process for functional auditors;

k.   Conducting education, training, research, and development efforts in the fields of supervision and the government internal control system;..."

BPKP is instrumental in developing government internal audit capabilities and encouraging training and professional development of government internal auditors throughout Indonesia.

---

[39] BPKP Strategic Plan 2015–2019.

[40] Ibid.

BPKP has established a Government Auditor Development Center and an Education and Training Centre to support its activities in this respect. By improving the competencies of government internal auditors, BPKP can help improve overall internal control competencies in their respective organizations.

BPKP has also promoted the establishment and development of the Association of Indonesian Government Internal Auditors (AAIPI), which is included in Government Regulation No. 60 of 2008 on the Government Internal Control System.

BPKP also acts as a partner to ministers, state ministries, institutions, local governments, and state-owned enterprises by providing them with assurance and consulting services.

In accordance with Article 38 of President Regulation Number 192 of 2014, the chairman coordinates with the minister/agency heads and local government chief executives "facilitating the development of the government internal control system, both in framework and implementation." Article 40 further states "In the performance of their duties, all elements in the BPKP are required to apply the principles of coordination, integration, simplification, and synchronization, both internally in the BPKP itself and in its relations with central and local government agencies."

Further, to support its own vision and mission "To be a World-Class Government Internal Auditor," BPKP conducted its own IA-CM Self-Assessment in 2015 and worked with the World Bank Group to perform an independent validation of that self-assessment. Having reached Level 3 – Integrated, BPKP has also developed a detailed action plan to improve the effectiveness and capability of other government internal audit offices in Indonesia to achieve Level 3 by 2019, as stipulated in Indonesian Medium Term Development National Planning documents.

B.1.3 Federative Republic of Brazil

The World Bank is supporting the Federative Republic of Brazil in establishing a modern system of internal control, which includes the function of professional internal auditing.

By way of background, there are three tiers of government in the Brazilian federation: the federal government, 26 states and the Federal District (in which the capital Brasília is located), and 5,570 municipalities.

The 1988 Federal Constitution is the main source document establishing the structure and mandates of the various control institutions in Brazil.

The Constitution requires the establishment of internal control entities to support public administrations in ensuring the existence of a strong internal control environment. The roles and responsibilities of the various control entities vary from state to state and within the federal domain. Some conduct compliance audits and checks, and/or financial and non-financial inspections or investigations. They may not necessarily conduct internal auditing as described in the *International Standards for the Professional Practice of Internal Auditing* or that expected from modern internal audit functions.

The Ministério da Transparência, Fiscalização e Controle – MTFC (Ministry of Transparency, Supervision and Control) is responsible for internal audit of Brazil's direct federal public administration in the Executive Branch. Internal audit is highly centralized within the MTFC, with each Ministry supported by a dedicated "internal audit division" within the MTFC. Some select organizations of the direct public administration have their own internal audit units (i.e., decentralized internal audit service or CISET). Organizations of the indirect public administration (e.g., agencies, foundations, state-owned and mixed-capital enterprises) are required by law to establish their own internal audit units.

The states have established State Internal Control Agencies (*Controladorias Gerais do Estado, CGEs*) but their capacities and modes of operation differ.

Some municipalities have also established Internal Control Agencies (*Controladorias Gerais do Municipios, CGMs*).

These Internal Control Agencies at the federal (MTFC), state (CGEs) and municipal levels (CGMs) have grouped together under an association (Conselho Nacional dos Orgãos de Controle Interno, CONACI) that seeks to enhance collaboration among the entities and to promote a closer integration of internal audit and control practices.

In May 2014, a Working Group composed of representatives from CONACI and the World Bank was created to support the modernization of the Brazilian Internal Control system, and enhance the capacity of governance and control organizations and agencies.

In 2015, the working group used the IA-CM as a self-assessment tool to identify various CGEs' levels/stages of development and conformance with the definition of internal auditing promulgated by The IIA.

A training program was established to train auditors on using the IA-CM as a self-assessment tool. Several CGEs performed self-assessments, which were validated by their peers. An independent third-party review of those self-assessments was conducted and made recommendations to support the CGEs in developing practical action plans to improve their capability levels and the effectiveness of their IA activities.

A seminar was held in May 2015 to highlight the results of the IA-CM assessments and move forward in strengthening internal auditing. Common themes that could be replicated to improve CGEs' capacities throughout Brazil were identified and discussed. CONACI working groups were proposed to address some of those themes.

Also at that seminar, a letter of commitment was signed to establish a working group composed of representatives from CONACI, MTFC, the Association of Audit Courts of Brazil (ATRICON), TCU, the Civil House of the Presidency, the Ministry of Planning, Budget and Management, the Ministry of Finance, and the Group of State Finance Managers (GEFIN), with advice from the World Bank, to identify the actions, activities, and components necessary to strengthen the internal control system in Brazil.

Further to its capacity building efforts, in March 2016, the World Bank organized a Brazil – Croatia and Bulgaria Knowledge Exchange Visit. Twelve Brazilian government officials participated and were hosted by government teams in Croatia and Bulgaria. Through this knowledge exchange, participants increased their understanding of the reform implementation issues faced in Croatia and Bulgaria and the strategies used to overcome those challenges, and had a better appreciation of the reforms/changes required, in order to improve the internal control system and internal audit function in the Brazil public sector.

In May 2016, to further support capacity building, a three-day conference focusing on Strengthening the Brazilian Public Sector Internal Control System was held in Brasília, Brazil.

The results of the Knowledge Exchange Visit were disseminated and the Conference helped instil a sense of purpose, commitment and ownership among key stakeholders and enhance a collective understanding of an envisioned reform—to change the current centralized system into a state-of-the-art public internal control system based on decentralized management under managerial responsibility (in line with international frameworks, standards and guidance; e.g., COSO, IPPF and INTOSAI).

The World Bank continues to support CONACI, identifying areas of mutual interest to work together.

B.1.4 East Africa

During the initial validations of the IA-CM (then referred to as the IA-CMM), central governments of three East African countries participated: Kenya, Tanzania, and Uganda.

They continue to use the IA-CM.

In Uganda, the government has included the IA-CMM in the Internal Audit Strategic Plan for the period 2015/16 to 2019/20 and it is considered key in guiding reform processes that are being undertaken.

The East African Community member states have adopted the model together with the IPPF in order to harmonize internal audit practices within the East African member states.

B.1.5 Office of the Auditor General, Asian Development Bank, Philippines

The Office of the Auditor General (OAG) at the Asian Development Bank (ADB) is committed to improving the capability of public sector internal auditors in Asia and the Pacific.

In August 2014, internal auditors from OAG participated in an IIA workshop to learn about the IA-CM for the Public Sector and use it to conduct a self-assessment of OAG.

Since that workshop, the OAG Capacity Development Working Group has developed a questionnaire using the IA-CM and The IIA's Global Internal Audit Survey for 2010 and 2015. The OAG plans to use that questionnaire as a tool for capacity development efforts requested by ADB public sector clients through ADB's regional departments.

Specifically, the IA-CM questionnaire enables public sector internal audit offices to assess their level of internal audit capability. Gaps between their current maturity and target maturity level are identified, and action plans to address these gaps are developed. The questionnaire will also gather baseline information on the demographics and institutional profile of the internal audit offices and the public sector organizations they serve. This was initially rolled out to the Association of Southeast Asian Nations (ASEAN) Central Bank Heads of Internal Audit Network.

Further to that initial questionnaire, an academic study, *Insights from the Study of Internal Audit Function in Selected ASEAN Central Banks*, was published by ADB in February 2017. The study examined the maturity of the internal audit function in the member states of the ASEAN by benchmarking the function with the IA-CM to understand the current capabilities of the internal audit function and the steps needed to enhance its capabilities.

In addition, selected public sector internal audit offices will be trained on the IA-CM model for the public sector and/or other suitable internal audit topics, as determined by the IA-CM questionnaire. OAG has also launched the AuditWithoutWalls!, a knowledge-sharing initiative which aims to create an online community of learners through a series of micro e-learning courses on internal audit topics, including the IA-CM.

B.2 Internal Assessment (Standard 1311)

B.2.1 Northern Health, British Columbia, Canada

Since 2010, the IA activity at Northern Health has applied the IA-CM to facilitate the performance of its Quality Assurance and Improvement Program, through a periodic Quality Assurance Review (QAR), further to Standard 1311–Internal Assessments.

Northern Health is one of five geographic health authorities and one provincial health authority providing all health care in the province of BC: acute care (hospitals), residential care, public health (prevention and protection), mental health, and addictions services. These are very complex and diverse organizations. The health authorities are governed by independent boards of directors appointed by the provincial government.

Northern Health's region covers the northern two thirds of BC, an area the size of France. BC's north has many geographic challenges: the Authority serves a population of only 300,000, scattered across this area. The facilities range from a medium-sized regional and teaching hospital to smaller hospitals, diagnostic and treatment centres, and community services offices. Some communities served are a significant driving distance from larger population centres, and some can only be reached by small plane or boat.

The IA activity was established in July 2004. It currently consists of a CAE plus one other auditor.

A periodic and regular QAR is undertaken to:

- Assess the existing IA capabilities against a comprehensive framework of leading practices in the profession of internal auditing;

- Identify significant gaps;

- Evaluate the importance to the organization of the capabilities not currently present in Northern Health Internal Audit;

- Provide the CEO and Audit and Finance Committee (AFC) with adequate information to evaluate and remediate or accept the corresponding risks to the organization;

- Develop a road map for required and desired improvement, taking into account the organization's complexity, operational risk, environment, and maturity; and

- Comply with professional standards.

The CAE uses the results of the IA-CM assessment when reporting to the board. It helps the AFC of the board understand the limitations of the IA activity and related risks, and familiarizes them with The IIA's *Standards* and leading practices.

The Northern Health IA activity has tailored the IA-CM to effectively use the model in its organization and environment. In this respect, there are some KPAs that may never be fully institutionalized in view of resource challenges, and these are clearly noted in the reporting to the board. In addition, two of the KPAs are not applicable within Northern Health's environment.

With respect to the first found in Level 5, "Public Reporting of IA Effectiveness,"[41] the accountability of the Health Authority is to the government, not to the population. Accordingly, the public is not considered an external stakeholder of the IA activity.

The second area relates to several KPAs, found in the element "Organizational Relationships and Culture," where the IA activity is expected to liaise/coordinate with the external auditor. The Northern Health IA services are risk-driven, and the non-financial risks in a healthcare environment normally far outweigh the financial risks. There is minimal overlap between IA's work and that of the external auditors. The IA activity and the external auditor compare plans and share information, but the actual coordination of the external auditor's work is conducted by senior leadership in finance.

B.2.2 International Development Research Centre (IDRC), Ontario, Canada

A Canadian Crown corporation and part of Canada's global affairs and development efforts, the International Development Research Centre (IDRC) invests in knowledge, innovation, and solutions to improve lives and livelihoods in the developing world. In the 2015–2016 fiscal year, IDRC had CA$263.1 million in revenues, nine donor partners, 675 projects, and 390 employees located in Ottawa, Canada; Cairo, Egypt; New Delhi, India; Nairobi, Kenya; and Montevideo, Uruguay.

In 2014, the internal audit (IA) activity at IDRC applied the internal audit capability model (IA-CM) to prepare for an external quality assessment. IDRC continues to use IA-CM as an integral part of its Quality Assurance and Improvement Program (QAIP), establishing an annual self-assessment program that conforms with Standard 1311 - Internal Assessments.

The IA activity comprises an auditor and a chief audit executive (CAE) and uses a co-sourcing model to support its services. The IA activity reports functionally to the Finance and Audit Committee (FAC) and administratively to the president.

In conducting the IA-CM self-assessment, the IA activity follows a fairly structured process that includes planning, fieldwork, and reporting, with the objective of determining and achieving the capability level appropriate for IDRC. The capability level is determined by applying professional judgement and seeking input from the FAC and senior management. Following this exercise, a current state assessment is completed and results are compared to essential activities, outputs, outcomes, and institutionalizing practices for each key process area. Recommendations and an action plan to address identified gaps are then developed. Results are reported by completing a color-coded IA-CM matrix to visually depict the internal audit capability level.

The IA-CM adds value as a communication tool, self-assessment tool, and performance improvement tool. It enables communication with the FAC and senior management and it provides a precedent for effective internal

[41] In this revised edition, this KPA has been changed to take into consideration IA activities where public reporting is not relevant and has been renamed "Outcome Performance and Value to the Organization Achieved."

auditing and how it can serve the organization. Senior management quickly recognized its value because the model originated from a credible source, it clearly identifies several capability levels that can be adopted to meet the needs of an organization, and it is especially useful for individuals who do not have a prior understanding of internal auditing.

As a self-assessment tool, the IA-CM assesses capabilities of internal audit against the expectations of senior management and the FAC, as well as supporting conformance with Standard 1311 - Internal Assessments. Although the first assessment using this model was time-consuming, it resulted in an in-depth analysis and the creation of useful measurement and reporting tools. Once the initial investment of time and effort to use the model was complete and tools were in place, future assessments were simple and straightforward.

The IA-CM is also a performance improvement tool. It allows the IA activity to easily determine areas that require improvement and helps determine an appropriate action plan. Recommendations from the eternal quality assessment were cross-referenced with the action plan to ensure thorough improvement efforts. A report summarizing these efforts and benefits, along with the color-coded matrix, is presented to the FAC and senior management annually. This information is used to assess the performance of the IA activity and the CAE.

The IA-CM has proven to be an invaluable tool that has improved the IA activity by ensuring its capabilities are aligned with the organization's expectations. As a result, the IA activity's ability to provide value to the organization through its audit and advisory engagements is improved, and is strongly supported by the FAC and senior management.

B.3 Visioning and Communication Tool

Audit committees appreciate having a clear understanding and vision of the state of the IA activity. The IA-CM provides a discussion framework for allowing the audit committee to select the level at which its IA activity can operate with a full appreciation of the limitations each level offers. The IA-CM can also help develop the road map for achieving a particular level, to be agreed upon by the responsible parties.

B.3.1 Fortune 500 Retailer, United States

The article, "Discover a Powerful Tool to Enhance Your Audit Strategy," in the July 2010 issue of The IIA's Internal Audit Foundation Report, highlighted how the IA-CM for the public sector was being adapted by CAEs in other industries as a powerful tool for developing an overall strategy, allowing CAEs to convey their vision to senior management and the audit committee. The article specifically described how the CAE at a *Fortune 500* retailer was using the IA-CM as a visioning and dialoguing tool.

At that time, the IA activity had developed an Internal Audit Capability/Maturity Projection table. The table demonstrated a plan to move to Level 5 (Optimizing) in three to four years where the priority in 2010 was to fill the gap at Level 3 (Integrated) and to get to level 4 (Managed) in terms of performance management and accountability. From there, it was easier to develop coordinated tactics in each of the other IA-CM elements with a clear understanding about how they will impact and improve the overall IA activity.

The CAE at that *Fortune 500* retailer continues to use the IA-CM. She now integrates the 25 core attributes from the "Capabilities of a World-Class Audit Function"[42] into the IA-CM.

Slides 1 and 2 are excerpts from a current internal audit department update to the audit committee.

As demonstrated by the following slides, the visual of the assessment can be compelling and is easy to present to the audit committee.

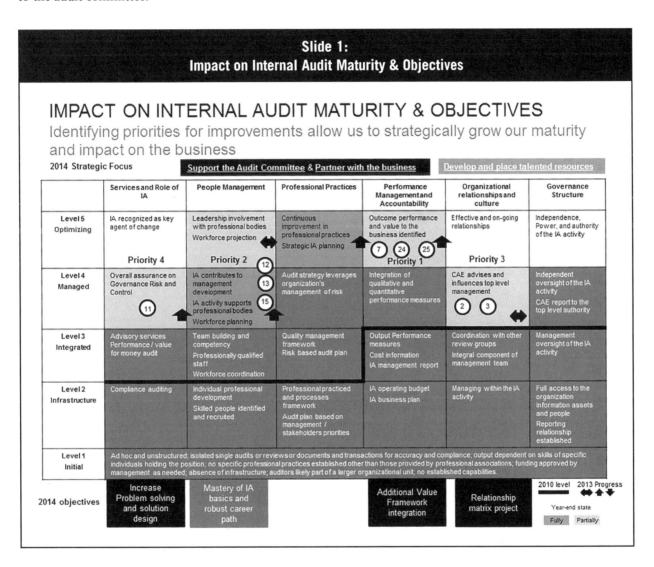

---

[42] Finance and Strategy Practice, Audit Director Roundtable, Corporate Executive Board.

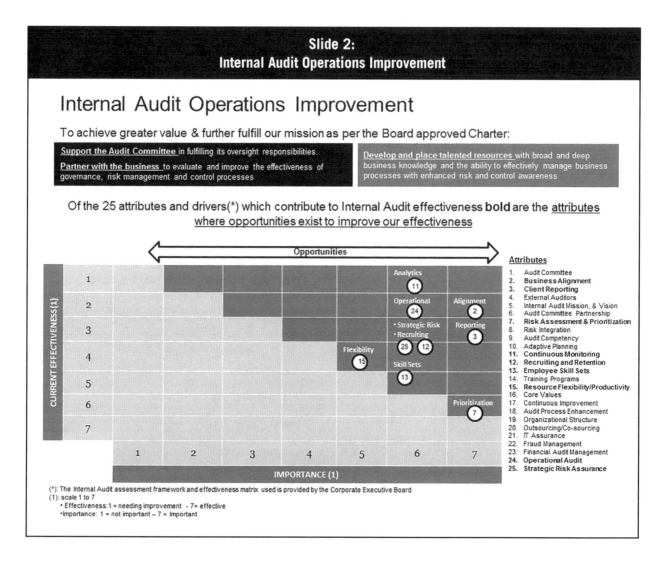

B.3.2 British Columbia Lottery Corporation, Canada

As a Crown Corporation, British Columbia Lottery Corporation (BCLC) conducts and manages lottery, eGaming, bingo, and casino gambling entertainment in a socially responsible manner for the benefit of British Columbians. For 31 years, more than $19 billion generated by BCLC gambling activities have been invested in health care, education, and community groups across B.C.

The internal audit department at BCLC consists of a director, three managers and six auditors. The department functionally reports to the audit committee and administratively to the CEO.

Internal audit started using the IA Capability Model during the latter part of 2011 and continues to revisit it annually. Initially, it was used as a starting point to provide a baseline assessment of the department and initiate discussions. Internal audit reviewed the six elements and various key process areas in an unstructured manner to subjectively assess the levels internal audit believed it had achieved. Subsequently, the model was used as an educational tool to communicate internal audit's current state and help clarify the key areas to focus on to reach its desired future state. This involved developing a road map that laid out the next two to three years of activities.

The benefits gained in using this tool can be grouped into three main components.

1. **Board and Audit Committee**
   - Alignment
   - Best-in-class strategy
   - Communication tool
   - Evaluation tool
   - Insight to what IA does

2. **CEO and Executive Management**
   - Helped changed the perception of the IA department
   - Alignment with executive group
   - Evaluation tool

3. **Internal Audit Staff**
   - Getting buy-in for department vision/strategy
   - Communication tool
   - Uniting the team
   - Task orientation
   - Personal development goal alignment

The details of the elements and key process areas of the IA Capability Model provided a step-by-step guide on how to move up the maturity model levels and helped the internal audit department focus its activities on value add and cost benefit areas.

B.4 Strategic Planning

The IA-CM can be used by the IA activity, management, and stakeholders to determine the capability level appropriate for the organization's oversight needs. In this way, the IA-CM can help align the current and future needs and expectations of management and stakeholders with the capabilities of the IA activity and resources available.

As a strategic planning tool, a similar process to that of a self-assessment is initially followed. However, when using the IA-CM as a strategic planning tool, it is also important to determine the requirements for the IA activity according to the organization's nature, complexity, and associated risks of its operations as well as assess the business needs of the organization. Any significant gaps between those requirements and the existing IA capabilities are identified. The organization must determine the highest level of capability to support its needs based on the resources available. The organization must make a commitment to achieve and maintain that desired level of capability.

In its 2016 report, *State of the Internal Audit Function in the United Nations System*, the United Nations Joint Inspection Unit states that "A good practice observed in a few organizations in the United Nations system, including UNRWA and WFP, and also in the Organisation for Economic Co-operation and Development (OECD), was the use of the IIA Internal Audit Capability Model as a means of gauging the desired level of maturity of the internal audit function. Determining the desired maturity level can guide the development of the internal audit strategy." (Paragraph 84, page 20)

B.4.1 The Organisation for Economic Co-operation and Development (OECD), Paris, France

"Better Policies for Better Lives"—the mission of the Organisation for Economic Co-operation and Development (OECD), an international organisation based in Paris, France—promotes policies that will improve the economic and social well-being of people around the world.

Part of the OECD Directorate for Internal Audit and Evaluation, internal audit (IA) comprises, besides the director (the CAE), two professional staff, and one audit and administrative assistant. IA has a dual reporting to the organisation's secretary-general (CEO) and to its audit committee.

This small and dedicated team achieved the highest rating in an External Quality Assessment (EQA) in 2015 (the third successive). As part of its preparation for this exercise, and in collaboration with the author of the model, Ms. Elizabeth MacRae, IA used the internationally recognized IIA Internal Audit Capability Model for the Public Sector (IA-CM). For each of the six elements of internal auditing, it assessed key performance areas institutionalized and in progress, and determined that it had, for the most part, achieved Capability Level 3 – Integrated, and defined areas for improvement. These planned improvements comprise the foundation of the "OECD Internal Audit Strategy 2015–2018," which is ambitious and aims to place IA near the top of the IA-CM by the end of 2018, whereby internal audit is recognized as a catalyst for positive change in OECD's governance, risk management, and control processes, and as a valued advisor. To do this, it "audits what matters" by providing assurance and advice at the corporate level and close to the substance of OECD's work.

B.4.2 Teacher Retirement System of Texas, United States

The IA activity of the Teacher Retirement System of Texas (TRS) uses the IA-CM for its strategic planning.

TRS administers a pension plan for 1.4 million participants, invests assets of $130 billion, and administers two of the largest health plans in the state. A staff of 12 internal auditors audits all aspects of the organization, including its strategic, operational, financial, and compliance risks. Internal audit reports directly to the audit committee of the board of trustees.

In 2010, the internal audit team identified a desire to develop a strategic plan. When the IA-CM was published, the team determined that it was a natural fit for assessing the IA activity's "as is" state and preparing for the "to be" state and the related road map (the strategic plan). In January 2011, the IA activity held an offsite retreat with staff, facilitated by human resources, to make these assessments and agree on the core elements of the plan. The plan is refreshed every two years.

The following are some benefits of using the IA-CM:

Collaboration and understanding among staff. The exercise was highly collaborative and the IA activity came away with a strong sense of mission and direction. The last external quality assurance review indicated that the strategic plan was well understood by staff and appeared to drive the IA activity's tactical decisions and audit plan.

Incorporation of audit activities into the organization's strategy. As the organization updated its strategic plan, the IA activity was able to make a link from its strategic plan to that of the organization. The IA activity is now included in the organization's strategic plan.

A tool for educating newer staff to internal audit and refreshing the rest of us. The IA activity uses the IA-CM to train staff on the expectations of the audit function and refresh the strategic plan every other year.

A tool for educating trustees and the public. The IA activity's strategic plan is included in its annual report and is posted on its website.

The IA activity has found that the IA-CM tool is a great one for orienting new trustees and executives to internal audit. Additionally, both groups have expressed a desire to see continuous improvement in the audit area and this tool is a way to demonstrate that by showing the progression from year to year. Reaction has been extremely positive and supportive across the board. The IA activity audit team is highly regarded, and using this tool is one of the reasons why.

B.4.3 School Employees Retirement System (SERS) of Ohio, United States

In 2016, the IA activity at the School Employees Retirement System (SERS) of Ohio initially applied the IA-CM to help in preparing its strategic plan for continuous process improvement. In addition, the IA-CM was helpful in readying internal audit activities for an upcoming external quality assessment. The CAE's Quality Assurance and Improvement Program (QAIP) utilizes the multiyear strategic plan as an ongoing mechanism to align internal audit activities with Standard 1311 - Internal Assessments.

SERS is a U.S. statewide defined benefit plan that provides retirement, disability, survivor benefits, and access to health care for eligible non-teaching employees of Ohio's public schools and community colleges. A Retirement Board of Trustees is responsible for the general administration and management of the system, and daily operations are administered by a professional staff led by the executive director. In the 2015–2016 financial year, SERS had $12.46B assets under management, nearly 123,000 active members, almost 74,000 retirees, over 1,000 contributing employer organizations, and 181 employees.

A new CAE was selected in 2015 and the self-assessment was seen as an orderly means of maturing the IA activity. The IA activity solely consists of a CAE and uses The IIA's Three Lines of Defense audit coordination model, as well as outsourcing to augment audit resources. The CAE reports functionally to the Retirement Board's Audit Committee (AC) and administratively to the executive director.

In conducting its IA-CM self-assessment, the IA activity followed a fairly structured process, which included planning, fieldwork, and reporting, to determine and achieve the capability level appropriate for SERS. The capability level was determined by applying professional judgment and seeking input from the AC and senior management. Following that exercise, a current state assessment was completed and results were compared to essential activities, outputs, outcomes, and institutionalizing practices for each key process area. Future strategies were identified to address gaps. Results were reported by completing a color-coded IA-CM matrix to visually depict the internal audit capability level.

The IA-CM adds value as a communication tool, self-assessment tool, and performance improvement tool. It enabled the IA activity to easily communicate and discuss with senior management and the AC what was meant by effective internal auditing and how it can serve the organization. It was especially useful for individuals possessing less understanding of internal audit. Because the model originated from a credible source and it clearly lays out different capability levels that can be adopted to meet the needs of an organization, senior management quickly saw the value in using it.

As a self-assessment tool, the IA-CM assesses capabilities of internal audit against the expectations of the CAE, senior management, and the AC, as well as supporting conformance with the *Standards*. The initial assessment using this model was fairly time-consuming, but resulted in an in-depth analysis and the creation of useful measurement and reporting tools. The IA-CM detailed a number of key activities that need constant attention to maintain a high maturity level. With those key activities identified and a repeatable IA-CM framework in place, future assessments will be easier to complete. An initial investment in time and effort definitely paid off for the future.

Lastly, it's a performance improvement tool. The self-assessment easily identified areas that required improvement and helped the CAE to implement a future strategic course of action.

An annual report summarizes and reports progress toward attainment of these future strategies and will be presented to the AC and senior management annually. This information will be useful in assessing the performance of the IA activity and the CAE. The IA-CM has proven to be an invaluable tool that will improve the IA activity by ensuring its capabilities are aligned with the organization's expectations. As a result, the IA activity is better able to provide value to the organization through its audits and advisory engagements and is strongly supported by the AC and senior management.

B.5 Benchmarking

The IA-CM can be used as a source of benchmarks by management, stakeholders, and policy centers. Through identification of selected KPAs and the practices institutionalized in that KPA, the level of capability/maturity in each IA element can be assessed by comparing practices of various organizations and jurisdictions.

B.5.1 The Internal Audit Foundation's Research Report "Internal Audit Capabilities and Performance Levels in the Public Sector" (2014)

The IA-CM was benchmarked against statistics from The IIA's 2010 Global Internal Audit Survey, which included 2,284 responses from public sector practitioners out of a total of 13,500 responses from 107 countries.

The study identified the survey questions where the public sector CAE responses would confirm performance or non-performance of a particular KPA or an essential practice supporting the achievement of that KPA identified in each of the six IA-CM elements. The study sought to answer the following questions:

- What are the most developed capabilities of public sector IA activities around the world?
- What areas are in most need of further development?
- What are the main regional differences?

The survey results were used to gauge the overall performance of public sector IA activities by each IA-CM element and capability level. This process created a global picture of the capability levels of public sector internal auditing for the first time. Highlights from the findings include:

- Most public sector IA activities stood at very low capability levels (Level 1- Initial and Level 2 - Infrastructure of the IA-CM).

- Most regions performed the essential practices best in the professional practices element.

- The United States and Canada region appeared to have the most advanced public sector IA activities compared to the other regions' survey responses.

- Most respondents indicated that their IA activities were seen as independent, objective assurance, and consulting activities.

- However, more focus needs to be placed on implementing more effective internal audit governance practices to support internal audit's independence, such as:
  o Establishing public sector audit committees, and
  o Involving the audit committee in CAE appointments.

- More effort is needed to ensure IA activities generally conform with the *International Standards for the Professional Practice of Internal Auditing* and implement a Quality Assurance and Improvement Program, including an external assessment.

Internal auditors and their stakeholders can use the results of this study to identify areas of strength and areas that need improvement to increase the effectiveness of their IA activities.

B.5.2 Malaysia Public Sector

Various research projects have been undertaken in Malaysia using the IA-CM to assess the capability of public sector internal audit activities. The three abstracts from published articles below reference the IA-CM assessments for three IA activities: at the state level, local government level, and a state statutory body.

"Importance of Internal Audit Capability in Management Accounting and Organisation Performance - A Case Study of Malaysian Public Sector Organisations"[43]

"This study specifically focuses on the role of internal audit in two different types of public sector entities: at a state level and a state statutory body. An explanatory case study method is used to collect the data whereby semi structured interviews, informal conversations, questionnaire and document reviews are conducted. It is found that the internal audit unit in Public Sector A obtained higher capability level of Level 2 (infrastructure) with overall percentage capability of 57 percent. Public Sector B only achieves level 5 (optimized) for the dimension of performance management and accountability. For the dimension of governance structure, Public Sector B achieves level 3 (integrated). The other three dimensions of services and role of internal auditing, professional practices, and organizational relationships and culture achieve level 2 (infrastructure). However, Public Sector B scores poorly for the people management dimension which is only level 1 (initial) which results in the overall capability of only level 1 (initial) with overall percentage of 52 percent. There is a critical need to review the dimensions of services and role of internal auditing, people management, and professional practices for both to enhance the effectiveness of the IA function. Implications and suggestions for further studies are also provided."

---

[43] Authors Hasnah Haron, Ishak Ismail, and Nur Ain Zakiah, University Malaysia Pahang, Malaysia, 2016; Presented at 10th New Zealand Management Accounting Conference (NZMA), "Extending the Boundaries of Management Accounting," November 24–25, 2016, Auckland, New Zealand.

"Assessment on Internal Audit Capability Level in a Public Sector Organisation"[44]

"This study serves to explore the level of capability of internal audit (IA) in a government agency in the public sector of Malaysia. Internal Audit Capability Model (IA-CM) from the Internal Audit Foundation was used as a basis to assess the capability level of IA. A series of interviews were conducted with the Ministry of Finance, Prime Minister's Department, Penang State Audit Department, and the IA department from a statutory body to better understand the public sector's structure, performance measurement systems, and applicability of IA-CM in the public sector. IA-CM evaluation shows a strong establishment in the elements of Services and Role of IA and Organizational Relationships and Culture, scoring a capability level of 4 or 5. There is a need to review the remaining elements (People Management, Professional Practices, Performance Management and Accountability, and Governance Structures) which were evaluated at capability level 2 or 3 to enhance the effectiveness of the IA function in the related government agency. The IA-CM model could be used as an assessment tool to serve as a common communication vehicle within the country as well as globally."

"Assessment on Internal Audit Capability Level in a Public Sector Organisation, Case Study on a Local Government"[45]

"This study serves to explore the level of capability of internal audit (IA) in a government agency in the public sector of Malaysia. Internal Audit Capability Model (IA-CM) from the Internal Audit Foundation was used as a basis to assess the capability level of IA. A series of interviews were conducted with the Ministry of Finance, Prime Minister's Department, Penang State Audit Department, and the IA department from a local government to better understand the public sector's structure, performance measurement systems, and applicability of IA-CM in the public sector. IA-CM evaluation shows a strong establishment in the elements of Services and Role of IA and Organizational Relationships and Culture, scoring a capability level of 4 or 5. There is a need to review the remaining elements (People Management, Professional Practices, Performance Management and Accountability, and Governance Structures), which were evaluated at capability level 2 or 3 to enhance the effectiveness of the IA function in the related government agency. The IA-CM model could be a centralized assessment tool to serve as a common communication vehicle within the country as well as globally."

---

[44] Authors Hasnah Haron, Ishak Ismail, Yuaraj Ganesan, Fathyah Hashim, and Aireen Mak Siew Fern, published in *Keeping in Touch*, The Institute of Internal Auditors Malaysia, Issue 02/2016, April – June 2016.

[45] Authors Hasnah Haron and Ishak Ismail, Faculty of Industrial Management, University Malaysia Pahang, Aireen Mak Siew Fern, Graduate School of Business, University Science Malaysia, Penang, Malaysia, published in Issue 1, Journal of Auditing in the Public Sector, p. 1–24, 2016.

INTERNAL AUDIT FOUNDATION
SPONSOR RECOGNITION

STRATEGIC PARTNER

Crowe Horwath

PARTNERS

PRESIDENT'S CIRCLE (US $25,000+)

Larry Harrington
CIA, QIAL, CRMA

Foundation Partners
(US $5,000–$14,999)

Wayne G. Moore
CIA

131

132